Teatime Stories for Mothers

Refreshment and Inspiration
to Warm Your Heart

Compiled by
Linda Evans Shepherd

RIVER
OAK
PUBLISHING

Teatime Stories for Mothers:
Refreshment and Inspiration to Warm Your Heart
ISBN 1-58919-593-0
Copyright © 2001 by Linda Evans Shepherd

Published by RiverOak Publishing
P.O. Box 700143
Tulsa, Oklahoma 74170-0143

Dedication

Dedicated to all the moms in my life:

Verna, Dorothy, Faith, Rebecca, Sharon W., Barb,
Bonnie, Kristina, Robin, Kim, Carey, Janet, Linda R.,
Jackie, Lisa, Luann, Sharon F., Pam, Margy, Clare,
Betty, Julie, Mildred, Karen, Shawna, Debbie, Marcia,
and so many others!

You are wonderful!

You are family!

You have helped me in
so many ways!

Thank You!

Introduction

Welcome to my tea party especially for mothers, grandmothers, and mothers-to-be.

Let me pour you a cup of steaming tea in a delicate china cup. I'll pass around a plate of warm scones topped with lemon curd and raspberry jam as you meet the special women I have invited.

We will laugh together as we share stories such as Nancy Kennedy's hilarious adventure in motherhood, "The Great Cart Caper." We may shed a few tears as we are touched by stories like Joy Shelton's "Love Conquers All." We'll bask in the warmth of cherished memories shared in "Is It Too Late" by Deborah Raney, and in many other heartwarming accounts.

Relax as we take turns telling the stories of our mothers, grandmothers, children—our friends and our lives. My hope is that you will be touched forever by these stories for and about mothers of all ages.

The tea's ready! Shall I pour?

Your hostess,

Linda Evans Shepherd

Tea Time Stories for Mothers

Table of Contents

A Mother's Love

*We find delight in the beauty and
happiness of children that makes
the heart too big for the body.*

Ralph Waldo Emerson

The Bread of Love

Bert Clompus

Children's children are a crown to the aged,
and parents are the pride of their children.

Proverbs 17:6

When I was a kid, Friday was always special. It was the day Mom baked fresh bread for the family. I'd run home from school and hang around her kitchen just to smell the sweet dough as it turned into golden loaves of bread.

One Friday, I pointed to her old-fashioned gas oven with its vault-like, porcelainized-steel door and said, "I know I can smell it, but how do I know there's really bread in there?"

Mom looked a bit surprised. "If you can ask a philosophical question like that, you must be growing up," she said with a twinkle in her eye. "But I'll tell you, it's a matter of faith—like believing in God. You can't see Him, but you know He's there, always loving you, always watching over you."

Then came the Friday I really learned about God's love. Dad came upon hard times, and a serviceman from the gas company came to shut off our gas because the bill hadn't been paid. I knew it was humiliating for Mom to open the oven door and show the serviceman the still-uncooked dough lying in the two glistening bread pans.

"Would you please wait a little while before turning off the gas, so my family can have bread tonight?" she implored.

The serviceman dropped his head and mumbled, "Sure, lady." Red-faced, he walked from Mom's little kitchen, climbed into his truck, and waited.

An hour later, the serviceman came back and walked down to the cellar. Mom and I heard the cold clank as he attached his wrench to the gas valve and turned it off. When he came upstairs, he grimly approached Mom. "I have something for you," he said and then handed her a bill. "When it's paid, I'll come back and turn on your gas."

Mom smiled and folded the bill carefully. She put it in the pocket of her apron and said, "I have something for you too."

She picked up a carefully wrapped package and handed it to the serviceman. It was a warm loaf of fresh-baked bread. The serviceman's face lit up. "Thank you," he said, "and God bless you."

That was years ago. And now, when I look down at Mom lying in her hospital bed, I long to talk to her, but she can't speak. I want to tell her how much I love her, but she can't hear. Only her hands let me know she still thinks of me. They move, gently massaging my hands, reminding me of the days she kneaded her dough with love.

Dear Lord, You gave me great riches when You gave me my mother. She gave so much of her life to raise me to be the person that I am. Bless her for all she's given to me, for a good family and upbringing are a person's greatest wealth. Amen.

Hat Hair

Donna Braymer

*The LORD is in his holy temple; the LORD
is on his heavenly throne. He observes
the sons of men; his eyes examine them.*

Psalm 11:4

We had hardly seen the top of our sixteen-year-old son's head for two years. This was because he wore an Astro's ball cap everywhere he went. For a while, he even slept in it because, he said, "It keeps my hair in place!"

When he ran in a cross-country race, the hat stayed on until it was time for the starting gun to fire. Then with a quick handover, he passed the hat to me. I held it, only until the race was over, then he plopped it back onto his head.

When the marching band performed during halftime at the football games, he wore a fancy band hat complete with a plume. But the minute he was back in the stands, off went the plume and on went his trusty Astro's cap.

How I longed to see what my son was becoming as he grew and matured under that hat. Just this week, when he announced he had decided to look for employment, I was excited. *Yea!* I thought. *Maybe he can get a job that doesn't require a hat as part of the uniform.*

I could just picture him checking out each possible employer, "Sir, I only have one requirement, you *do* issue a company hat, right?"

But to my great pleasure, he was hired at a wonderful clothing store in the mall. He would have to dress up in a nice shirt, tie, and slacks. *Wonderful! No ball cap at work!*

Today, when he dressed for school, he popped on the hat. "You'll have hat hair if you wear that hat."

He said, "I don't care. I'll shower when I get home!"

I couldn't believe that my sixteen-year-old would rather bathe than give up his hat!

Yet after school when I saw him, squeaky clean, coming down the stairs for his first day of work, I had to look again. Was this my son? So quickly he had gone from a dirty-faced two-year-old, clutching a blanket in one hand and a ball in the other, to a man. It didn't seem possible. The dress shirt, tie, dress slacks, and nice shoes had transformed him. The orthodontist and braces had created a friendly smile, and, I noticed with pride, he also had beautiful brown hair.

I complimented him on how great he looked. His smile and "Ah, Mom" was enough for me!

I know the story doesn't end here. Someday a pretty, young lady will convince him to dress up and wait for her at the end of a church aisle. Even though I will be happy that the day has finally come, I will be sad to see the "hat hair" and blanket days gone forever.

Well, maybe not forever—perhaps my future grandson will find it necessary to don a ball cap.

Dear Lord, a child is a promise—a promise of hope, a promise of the future. Thank You for the wonderful child You have given me. I know he is mine to hold only for a little while. Help me to teach him how to become an adult, an adult who will be a blessing to all who know him. Amen.

A Time to Choose

Nancy Maffeo

She is a tree of life to those who embrace her;
those who lay hold of her will be blessed.

Proverbs 3:18

"No," Dana, my squirming two-year-old, said as she pushed away my attempt to hug her. I sighed, *Why is it always this way with her?*

My feeling of rejection turned into resentment. As I matched her socks, I mulled over our relationship. How I longed to feel her arms around my neck, to snuggle with her. But it never seemed to happen.

"Doggie, doggie," she cooed as she toddled toward me, waving her favorite book.

Irritated, I paused from my work. "Yes, Honey, it's your doggie book." I glanced at her and then pulled open a drawer to deposit folded clothes, as I mentally checked my long to-do list.

"Book, book," Dana insisted. Suddenly, she whacked it across my leg. I turned to yank it out of her hand when a thought fell into my heart: *God is never frustrated with my attempts to get His attention.*

My hand stopped in midair. Instead of grabbing the book from Dana's hand, I gently took it and carried her to the sofa. In a moment, she scrambled next to me, and we read it together.

Dana loved *Doggie*. She knew it by heart and could parrot most of the words on each page. After we read it through twice, I put it aside and returned to the clothes basket. A moment later Dana returned with another book.

"Not now," I said. However, even before the words crossed my lips, another thought slipped through my mind already prioritizing a revised list of things to do: *Read to her.*

With a weary sigh because I was already behind schedule and not likely to finish my self-assigned chores before dinner, I gave in to the urging. I dropped the towels back into the basket and carried Dana to the sofa. We read the new book, then a third. Then we read *Doggie* once more. By the time I finished, Dana was snuggled in my lap, pointing to her favorite pictures.

From that day on, things were different between us. Whenever (well, almost whenever) Dana wanted to spend time with me, I stopped what I was doing—if only for a few moments—and gave her my attention. Sometimes it was for just a minute to look at a toy. Sometimes we spent an hour reading, blowing bubbles, or having "tea" with her dolls. But over time, my squirming, reluctant child opened her heart and let me in.

Today, twenty years later, though separated by the miles, I wait for the ring of the phone and the e-mails that arrive every few days.

Dana knows she is never so far away, nor so old, that I won't take time when she calls or visits to listen, to laugh and to talk over a cup of tea.

Dear Lord, in the busyness of life, it's hard to stop for my children. Help me to seek and find opportunities to bless them with my time. For I have learned that giving my time to my children—or other children in my life—is one of the best investments I can make. Amen.

Love Conquers All

Joy Shelton

We will shout for joy when you are
victorious and will lift up our banners
in the name of our God. May the
LORD grant all your requests.

Psalm 20:5

My husband had just accepted the pastorate of a small church. When we moved, our oldest daughter, Debby, a social worker, came over for the weekend. She told us about her encounters with children who needed loving, stable homes. She said, "Mom and Dad, why don't you become foster parents?"

"Us? That's impossible!" I told her. After all, two of our four children had already left home, and the two we had left were teenagers. We couldn't take in children!

But after Debby left, my husband and I could not get her challenge out of our minds.

We prayed and decided to turn in our application. We knew just what we wanted—one child, an older child, perhaps a ten-year-old.

Three weeks passed and the phone rang one morning while I was vacuuming the carpet. It was a child-welfare officer with a crisis. "We have a little girl, six months old, and her eighteen-month-old brother who need immediate placement!"

"Oh no, we can't do that!"

"Would you at least think about it?"

"Okay, I'll talk to my husband. I'll call you in the morning."

I hung up, flustered. *How could I have promised to consider this? What a dilemma!*

My husband came home from the office late that afternoon, and we talked. Even though questions flooded our minds, we knew God must have opened this door.

The next morning I told the social worker, "We'll take the kids, but only on a trial basis."

She was thrilled. "Great! We'll bring the children tomorrow at 4:00 P.M. And by the way, the little guy loves Italian food."

The next day, I prepared the rooms for the children and I also made spaghetti for dinner—expecting two little dark-haired children to show up at our door.

That afternoon, a bright red Toyota pulled into our driveway. My eyes were riveted on the little cotton-top heads bobbing up and down in the backseat.

Our entire family fell in love with the children. Billy was an energetic, bright-eyed little boy with personality plus. His sister, Connie, was very subdued and was experiencing some developmental delays. Only that morning had they taken two casts off her frail little arms; it turned out that both children were victims of child abuse. We were horrified by the story the social worker told us.

Each day we grew more attached to Billy and Connie and would have adopted them had it been possible. I felt resentment toward their mother and father. *If I ever see them, I'll let them know what I feel about what they've done to these children!*

Two years later, Billy and Connie had grown and blossomed under our care. Billy loved to stand at the door of our little church with my husband and greet the congregation as they came in. He'd stick out his little hand and say, "I'm so happy you came to church today!"

Connie, with an enormous amount of attention and stimulation from our older children, thrived. At eighteen months, she took her first step!

One day, the social worker stopped by. He seemed very uncomfortable. "Billy and Connie will be going home to their mother and father in three days," he informed us.

We couldn't believe our ears! *We can't give up our children!*

We grieved. *Why had we allowed ourselves to be put in this situation? Why would God let Billy and Connie be returned to the parents who had hurt them?*

Three days later, the red Toyota appeared in our driveway. Our entire family had stayed home that day so that we could say good-bye. Reluctantly, we put their belongings in the car. As the car pulled away from the curb, Billy looked up and waved to us. It was a terrible moment.

Later, when I tried to pray, God seemed too far away. I simply could not understand. Still, our church family prayed for Billy and Connie . . . and their parents. We asked God to send them some caring people who would make a difference.

And though we were not allowed to have any contact with the children, the social worker told us that my husband and I could send cards or small gifts to them through the Child Welfare office.

Shortly before Valentine's Day, we sent a package of love gifts to the children. But for some reason, this particular package slipped through the welfare system without the return address being removed. Then the day after Valentine's Day, the phone rang.

"Hello?"

"This is Billy and Connie's mother."

I almost gasped.

She asked, "Would you like to come over for a visit?"

On that visit, we learned that the children's father had been in prison and both parents were the products of abusive foster homes. They had been so mistreated and had never been loved by anyone or learned how to love others.

The resentment and hatred I had felt toward them melted away. In its place, I felt love for the entire family.

We established a relationship with the parents, and over a period of time, they began attending our church. We were now Billy's and Connie's "aunt" and "uncle" and were once again privileged to be a part of their lives and to enjoy their antics.

I was ecstatic. God had heard and answered our prayers. We had prayed for God to send a caring family, and He had sent us! What grace.

Although many lessons have been learned through this experience, one stands out. Never underestimate the power of the Heavenly Father. He works all things together for good to those who love Him and are called according to His purpose.

Dear Lord, You are in control! I'm so glad it's not up to me but up to You. I give You my life and ask You to guide me one step at a time. I may not be able to see the end of the road, but I know that You can. Thank You for authoring our adventure! Amen.

The Best Gift

Linda Evans Shepherd

*Though I speak with the tongues of men
and of angels, but have not love, I have
become sounding brass or a clanging cymbal.
And though I have the gift of prophecy,
and understand all mysteries and all
knowledge, and though I have all faith,
so that I could remove mountains,
but have not love, I am nothing.*

1 Corinthians 13:1-2 NKJV

What's the most important gift a person can give?
My daughter gives it often, even though she has to sit
in a wheelchair and does not have the ability to speak.

Sometimes I get tired of dealing with well-meaning
people who inquire about her. Usually I'm in a group

of women when a conversation starts with the casual question, "Do you have any children?"

I try to avoid saying I have a child who is handicapped, because the person asking the question is usually not ready to get emotionally involved with my problems.

But their original, "Do you have kids?" question is usually followed by, "What school does your daughter go to?"

Unfortunately, this probe seems to open the door to conversation chaos.

"Laura goes to two schools," I explain. "One for kids with special needs and one for typical kids."

"Special needs?" I'm asked. "Is your daughter all right?"

Inwardly, I grimace. I've been down this road of explanation before, and I know what is about to happen.

"She's a happy little girl," I say. "But she's handicapped."

"What's wrong?"

"She was in a car accident when she was eighteen months old," I explain.

Shock wakes the person's features. Desperate to make Laura's situation all right, they ask, "But she's okay now, right?"

To me, this is a difficult question. Of course I think she's okay. I know she's only handicapped. I also know my interviewer won't understand that. So I say, "Well, Laura's in a wheelchair."

More desperate than ever, the person asks, "But she can talk and stuff, right?"

I sigh. There's no way out of this one. "No, but she can communicate with tongue signals."

By this time, my interviewer is at a loss for words. So, I try to help out. "But you know, Laura's a happy little girl who really enjoys her life."

The person nods mutely and steps back as if ready to make a run for it.

I step closer. "She really is a happy child. And she has lots of friends."

"Oh," my interviewer responds in a whisper. "She's lucky she has you for a mother."

I force a smile and say, "As far as I'm concerned, I'm just a mother who is lucky to have such a sweet kid for a daughter!"

My questioner excuses herself, and I'm left feeling unsettled. If only I could explain the validity of Laura's life in a way the casual conversationalist could understand. Unfortunately, our society is not taught to recognize the viability of a life that can offer nothing to the world except love.

I think the gift of love Laura so freely gives is worth more than any other gift that even an able-bodied person can offer. I have a child who not only receives love but radiates love to all those around her. I am a fortunate mother indeed.

Dear Lord, help me to recognize what is truly valuable in my life and the lives of the ones I love. Teach me to demonstrate my love in a way that will draw us closer together and draw us closer to You. Amen.

A Mother's Encouragement

Mother's are angels who
teach their children to fly.

Anonymous

i Can

Eva Marie Everson

*I can do everything through
him who gives me strength.*

Philippians 4:13

I was the quintessential "I can't" child; the poster child for the advancement of the word "can't." Whatever my mother told or asked me to do was immediately followed by my whining, "I caaaaan't." Consequently, very few tasks or goals that I set out to accomplish were ever completed.

One evening when I was seven, my mother called me into the family room where she was reading an article in the *TV Guide.* On the cover was a photo of Marlo Thomas, currently starring in the popular sitcom, *That Girl.* Mother knew that the show was one of my favorites, and Marlo one of my show-biz idols.

"I want you to read this article," Mother began. "It's about Marlo Thomas. She tells how a simple poem that her father forced her to learn changed her life. She went from saying, 'I can't,' to 'I can!' According to this article, she was able to change her life, and eventually her career, by learning the principles in the poem."

Sensing a conspiracy between Marlo Thomas and my mother, I took the small magazine and looked down at the glossy pages. There was Marlo, looking perky and adorable. Her smile was radiant and her trademark shoulder-flip hair was styled to perfection. I thought it must be grand to be Marlo! Beside her photo was the poem my mother had spoken of; a simple poem entitled, "I Can."

"I want you to memorize that poem," Mother said firmly.

"Mamaaaaa," I bellyached. "I can't learn that poem. It's too loooong."

"It's not too long and yes, you can learn it. I want you to know it perfectly by this time tomorrow."

One does not say no to my mother. She coined the phrase: "When I tell you to jump, you ask, 'How high?'" She was the queen of Dogwood Drive. I adored her, but this was going too far!

I slumped my shoulders, turned, and trudged my way back to my bedroom with the magazine loosely held in my small right hand. With a heavy heart, I plopped onto my bed, fell back against the cotton spread, and began my task. "Can't is a word that is foe to ambition," I began. I repeated the line. I repeated it again and again until it held firm in my heart. "An enemy ambush to shatter your will. . . ." I continued the process until the following evening, when I proudly recited the poem that has continued to be my motto.

Ms. Thomas did not know me, but her story forever changed my life. Saying "I can" helped me to survive the worst moments of my life. Saying "I can" encouraged me to accomplish things I would have otherwise seen as out of my reach. A simple poem learned at age seven is a poem that will sustain me to seventy-seven, maybe even longer.

I Can

Can't is a word that is foe to ambition;
An enemy ambush to shatter your will.
Its prey is forever a man with a mission;
It bows but to courage, and patience, and skill.
So hate it with hatred that's deep and undying,
For once it is welcomed 'twill break any man.
And whatever the goal you are seeking,
Keep trying!
And answer this demon by saying, "I can!"

—*Edgar A. Guest*

Dear Lord, I can do ALL things through You, because You strengthen me. Thank You that I am not called to be a success but to be faithful. For my faith is in You as I step out and follow You one step at a time. Through You, I can do anything! Amen.

Heaven's Treasure

Rosey Dow

*"A new commandment I give to you,
that you love one another; as I have
loved you, that you also love one another."*

John 13:34 NKJV

I wanted to hide behind Dave, my fiancé, the night he took me to meet his parents. His father was a pastor and his mother a Bible teacher. His parents had been missionaries. I knew I'd never measure up to their expectations.

I was a bus kid from the dysfunctional home of a foul-mouthed truck driver. What could I say to people who'd spent years in the ministry? Why was I so foolish to think they'd want someone like me marrying their son?

His mother met us in the front hall. She was a tall woman with a soft figure and twinkling blue eyes. "Welcome," she said. Her smile warmed my cold hands. "I'm so glad you came tonight." She sent her son a knowing smile and shared it with me. "I've heard so much about you."

The house had a cozy feeling, filled with love and children and the smell of fresh bread. My visit passed like a pleasant daydream. I giggled at his dad's sour jokes and laughed at his little brother's antics. We played Aggravation with the children until my smile muscles ached.

His mother hovered over us like gentle mist. She spoke little, but when she did, her words and warm looks wrapped around my hungry heart. I wanted the evening to last forever.

That night started a love affair as sweet and passionate as any romance. But this time it was between a young man's mother and me. I had feared that she'd expect things I couldn't give. Instead, she gave me things I'd never expected. I wanted to be near her every minute.

When Dave went back to college, she often asked me to go shopping, just the two of us. She bought me ice-cream cones and told me family stories that everyone else had long forgotten. She invited me for weekends of leisurely walks and intimate talks. She was a mentor, a confidante, a friend.

After our wedding, Dave and I lived near his parents, and I felt doubly blessed. Mom saved her change and bought matching lamps for our tiny living room. She took me shopping every Friday, but now we bought groceries. When the babies arrived one after the other, she came daily to help. Her presence brightened my weary afternoons. She never criticized my fumbling. All she offered was love.

Before our second child was a year old, an aneurysm took Mom to heaven. I was devastated. It seemed she'd only been mine for a few days. Why had God taken her from me so soon?

I struggled for weeks, doubting God's care, grieving for someone I loved. Then, God gave me the answer. He had given me a special treasure that few in life will know. No matter that I held it briefly, I was blessed to have had it even a few hours, a priceless gift of love that knows no end. It's now hidden in my heart.

Dear Lord, help me to see and appreciate the treasures You have placed in my life. For the treasure of my family and friends makes me very wealthy indeed. May I value these dear ones in a way that will profit our relationships. Amen.

Good Morning, I Love You!

Margie Seyfer

It is good to praise the LORD and make
music to your name, O Most High,
to proclaim your love in the morning.

Psalm 92:1-2

When I speak, I tell my audiences, "As you get out of bed each morning and stumble into the bathroom, do you see a vision of yourself in the mirror and scream? If you want to jump-start each day with a positive attitude, look in the mirror and say, 'Good Morning. I love you. We're going to have a great day!'"

Recently, Jill called to tell me how much she appreciated learning about my "Good morning" greeting. It worked so well on herself that she decided to try it on her family. She said, "Our Sunday scramble to church had become a war. It was a fight to get my family out of bed and dressed. Yet, despite all my ranting and raving, we always arrived late, surrounded by an angry cloud of silence.

"The next Sunday, I tried your affirmation. I stood over my husband's side of the bed and whispered in his ear, 'Good morning. I love you. We're going to have a great day!'

"He opened one eye and said, 'What? Are you crazy?'

"I just smiled and went across the hallway to our five-year-old son's bedroom. I opened the door and repeated the greeting. Jeff rolled over and said, 'You're wrong, Mom. We're going to have a bad day!'

"I smiled again and went across the hallway to check on Dan. I couldn't believe it, he was already up, dressing!

"I trotted back to Jeff's room. To my surprise he, too, was out of bed, putting on his clothes! That Sunday was the first in a month of Sundays we arrived to church on time, still liking one another."

Jill has turned this greeting into a morning ritual. She told me she had been especially worried about her son's negative attitude. She said, "Each morning, I would wake Jeff with my greeting, and each morning he would give me some sort of a cynical retort.

"But one morning, I opened his bedroom door, and before I could speak, he looked up at me with his big brown eyes and said, 'Good morning. I love you. We're going to have a great day!'"

Jill concluded by saying, "Since then, Jeff's negative attitude has vanished. You know, not only is it going to be a great day, it's going to be a great year! My family's nasty attitude has been replaced by a promising outlook! That has made all the difference."

When you look for a great day, you will find it.

Dear Lord, I know my attitude is the compass for the whole day. Please help me to face each day with cheer so that I may spread that cheer to others. Help me to sweeten, not to sour, my relationships. Amen.

Love Lives Forever

Peter Dow as told to Rosey Dow

Train a child in the way he should go, and when he is old he will not turn from it.

Proverbs 22:6

My mouth felt dry as I followed my mother into the doctor's private office and sank into a padded chair next to hers. This doctor didn't carry a stethoscope. He had a room full of gadgets and gizmos to analyze the learning abilities of failing students. That day he had analyzed me.

He shuffled papers and jabbed his wire-frame glasses with a forefinger. "I'm sorry to tell you this, Mrs. Dow, but Peter has dyslexia—a fairly severe case."

I swallowed and tried to breathe. The doctor went on. "He'll never read above the fourth-grade level. Since he won't be able to complete high-school requirements, I suggest you enroll him in a trade school where he can learn to work with his hands."

I didn't want to go to trade school. I wanted to be a preacher, like my dad. My eyes filled with tears, but I forced them back. A twelve-year-old was too big to cry.

Mom stood up, so I jumped to my feet too. "Thank you, Doctor," she said. "Come along, Peter."

We drove home without saying much. I felt numb. Dyslexia? I'd never heard the word until the previous week. Sure, I was always the slowest kid in my class. At recess I had a special hiding place behind a shrub where I would cry because I couldn't do my lessons, no matter how hard I tried.

Of course, I never told Mom that part about school. I was too ashamed. I did not want to worry her, either. She had enough on her mind with teaching school full time and caring for my two brothers, my sister, and me.

Mom and I arrived home before the rest of the family. I was glad. I wanted some time alone. With my chin almost touching my chest, I pulled off my coat and hung it in the closet. When I turned around, Mom was standing right in front of me. She didn't say anything. She just stood there, looking into my eyes with wet tracks down her cheeks. Seeing her cry was too much for me. Before I knew what was happening, I was in her arms, bawling like a big baby. A few minutes later, she led me into the living room to the couch.

"Sit down, honey. I want to talk to you."

I rubbed my eyes with my sleeve and waited, plucking at the crease in my trousers.

"You heard what the doctor said about your not finishing school. I don't believe him."

I stopped sniffling and looked at her. Her mild blue eyes smiled into mine. Behind them lay an iron will. "We'll have to work very hard, you and I, but I think we can do it. Now that I know what the problem is, we can try to overcome it. I'm going to hire a tutor who knows about dyslexia. I'll work with you myself evenings and weekends."

Her eyebrows drew down as she peered at me. "Are you willing to work, Peter? Do you want to try?"

A ray of hope shone through the hazy future. "Yes, Mom. I want to real bad."

The next six years were an endurance run for both of us. I studied with a tutor twice a week until I could haltingly read my lessons. Each night Mom and I sat at my little desk and rehearsed that day's schoolwork for at least two hours, sometimes until midnight. We drilled for tests until my head pounded and the print blurred before my eyes. Twice a week I wanted to quit. I felt as if I had only the strength of a kitten, but Mom's courage never wavered.

She'd rise early to pray over my school day. A thousand times I heard her say, "Lord, open Peter's mind today. Help him remember the things we studied."

Her vision reached beyond the three Rs. Twice I won at statewide speech competitions. I participated in school programs and earned a license to work as an announcer on a local radio station.

Then Mom developed chronic migraines during my senior year. She blamed the headaches on stress. Some days the intense pain kept her in bed. Still she'd come to my room in the evening, wearing her robe, an ice pack in her hand, to study with me.

We laughed and cried when I passed my senior finals. Two days before graduation, I talked to Mom and Dad about Bible college. I wanted to go, but I was afraid.

Mom said, "Apply at the Bible institute here in town. You can live at home, and I'll help you."

I put my arms around her and hugged her close, a baseball-size lump in my throat.

A week after graduation, Mom felt a stabbing pain in her head. She became disoriented for just a moment but seemed to be all right. It was another migraine, she thought, so she went to bed. That night Dad tried to wake her. She was unconscious.

A few hours later, a white-coated doctor told us Mom had an aneurysm that had burst. A massive hemorrhage left us no hope. She died two days later.

My grief almost drowned me. For weeks I walked the floor all night, sometimes weeping, sometimes staring at nothing. Did I have a future without Mom? She was my eyes, my understanding, my life. Should I still enroll in Bible school? The thought of going on alone filled me with terror. But, deep inside, I knew I had to move on to the next step, for her.

When I brought home the first semester's books and course outlines, I sat in the chair at my little desk. With trembling fingers, I opened my history book and began to read the first chapter. Suddenly, I looked over at the chair she used to sit in. It was empty, but my heart was full.

Mom's prayers still followed me. It was almost as though she was still there. I remembered her faith.

In my graduation testimony I said, "Many people had a part in making Bible college a success for me. The person who helped me most is watching from Heaven tonight. I wish I could say to her, 'Thank you, Mom, for having faith in God and faith in me. You will always be with me.'"

Dear Lord, thank You for women like Peter's mother who set fine examples for me. Help me to not only be a person my children can lean on but also one who can take a stand. Help me to reach out to my own children so that they can know the value of a good mother. Amen.

Inside Out

Carol McAdoo Rehme

I love the house where you live,
O LORD, the place where your glory dwells.

Psalm 26:8

Her world was shattered with the divorce.

Bills, house payments, health insurance. Her part-time job provided little income and fewer benefits. With no financial support, she finally lost the house.

At wit's end, Karen managed to rent a cramped camper at the local RV park for herself and five-year-old Joshua. It was only a little better than living out of their car, and she wished with all her heart that she could provide more for her child.

After their evening ritual of reading and playing a table game, Karen sent her son outside to play while she agonized over the checkbook. She glanced out the window when she heard voices.

"Say, Josh, don't you wish you had a real home?" asked the campground manager.

Karen tensed and held her breath as she leaned nearer the open window. Then a smile spread across her face when she heard Joshua's response.

"We already have a real home," he said. "It's just that we don't have a house to put it in."

Dear Lord, You are a God of miracles who can cause a small house to contain as much love as a large one. Help me to increase the love in my home by spending my time with my kids. Amen.

Special Moments

*The best thing to spend on
your child is your time.*

Anonymous

Monet's Sunrise

Mary van Balen Holt

*Satisfy us in the morning with your
unfailing love, that we may sing
for joy and be glad all our days.*

Psalm 90:14

"Mom, Mom!"

I turned over in my bed. Through sleepy eyes, I saw
a bleary image of my daughter, Kathryn, standing
beside me.

"Mom," she whispered again, "would you watch the
sunrise with me, like Monet did?"

My eyes began to focus. I could see the expectant
look on her face. She had become keenly interested in
Monet, his paintings, and all things French. That
particular morning, she had decided to get up early

and observe a sunrise from our front porch. She had invited me to share the experience. How could a mother refuse such an invitation? How often are we grown-ups included in such serendipitous moments? I am not an early riser. Sunsets are more compatible with my schedule. However, getting out of bed, I pulled on jeans and a T-shirt. We walked through the living room. I grabbed afghans for both of us, and together we stepped out onto the front porch.

We snuggled close in our blankets and leaned our backs against the house. In silence, we watched. Night's cold seeped from the concrete porch, chilling us through the afghans. Suddenly, the sky was painted with rose, pink, purple, and bright blue. In minutes, the colors moved across the sky. Still silent, we witnessed the common miracle.

This happens every morning, I thought to myself, *and I sleep through it!*

"How does he do it?" Kathryn asked. "How does Monet get the paint to look like this?"

We both sat awash in the morning's glory. When the sun was up and the sky was tame again, we went inside for a cup of tea.

Dear Lord, there is no way to describe the beauty of Your love. Even if I could paint as beautifully as Monet painted a sunrise, I could never capture the awesome majesty of Your love for my children or me. Thank You for surrounding me with such beauty. Amen.

The Happies!

Linda Evans Shepherd

The joy of the LORD is your strength.
Nehemiah 8:10

Sometimes, when happiness comes my way, I'm too preoccupied to notice.

One day, my then three-year-old son, Jimmy, and I ran some errands. I let him take his red and yellow tape recorder into the print shop. Standing next to the purring copy machine, I hadn't realized how loud Jimmy's Sesame Street sing-along tape blared. Suddenly, Jimmy turned the volume up and jumped from the floor. "Let's dance!" he shouted.

My eyes widened as I watched Jimmy gyrate, beckoning me to join his fun.

"Mommy's busy right now," I murmured. I turned my head to sneak a peak at the print-shop staff. *Were they watching the show?*

My mouth fell open. All the workers, owner included, were standing at their desks doing the twist to Jimmy's music!

I laughed at all the happiness around me. This time, I couldn't ignore Jimmy's glee.

The next time I hear a tune that calls for giddiness, I'll shout, "Let's dance!"

Will you join me?

Dear Lord, happiness is not based on my circumstances but on how I handle them. When I experience the beat of life, help me not to despair but to dance! For You are my rhyme and reason—You set the rhythm. May I see my world from Your perspective. Amen.

Is It Too Late?

Deborah Raney

*We loved you so much that we were
delighted to share with you not only
the gospel of God but our lives as well,
because you had become so dear to us.*

1 Thessalonians 2:8

As we get ready to pack up all the worldly
belongings of our oldest daughter and drive eight
hours to deposit her at college in another state, I feel a
vague sense of panic come over me. It has nothing to
do with her safety, her future, or even with how much
I'm going to miss her. She is one of the most mature,
levelheaded, delightful young women I know, and her
future is bright. She graduated at the head of her
class, excelled in sports and music, and was crowned

prom queen. I have no doubt that she'll have a host of friends after one week in the dorm.

It's a forgone conclusion that I'll miss her, just like I missed her older brother when he went away to college three years ago. I'm resigned to that.

No, my alarm comes from a sudden realization that we failed to give her the fairy-tale childhood I imagined for her. And now it's too late. Our chance is gone.

Growing up on a farm, I had that storybook childhood. Among my memories are playing in the sweet-smelling hayloft in the barn my great-grandfather built, searching for the newest batch of baby kittens, catching fireflies on a starry summer night, splashing in the cool pasture pond.

I wanted all of that for Tobi Anne. Even while I carried her in my womb, I dreamed of a fluffy pink cloud of a nursery and later a canopied bed and French Provincial furniture. I dreamed of a lush green lawn and the best toys money could buy; a wardrobe of frilly lace dresses and patent-leather Mary Janes to match each outfit. We would give her dancing lessons and fancy birthday parties, and we'd buy her a pony to ride.

She and I would read every *Little House on the Prairie* book together, side by side in a cozy room with a roaring fire, while we sipped hot cocoa and munched on animal crackers.

Her father and I would orchestrate her days so that every moment was destined to become a memory in her scrapbook. Nothing would be left unfinished.

But something happened along the way, and many things were left undone. By the time I got around to making time for the "Little House" books, she was reading well on her own. She finished every one of them alone in her room one summer.

We took her to a beginner's ballet class when she was four, but she was frightened by the other children, and we never went back. We couldn't have afforded the lessons for long anyway.

The birthday parties were always small family affairs with homemade cakes that never quite turned out like the pictures in the magazines. And instead of frilly pinafores and fancy shoes, she wore hand-me-downs from friends and even her big brother's outgrown jeans and tennis shoes.

The cozy house with the fireplace turned out to be a crowded duplex and a lawn with a view of the neighbor's junk pile; and instead of a pony, Tobi loved a succession of scruffy cats.

My husband reminds me that this thing that happened along the way—this thing that kept my fantasies from becoming reality—is called life. He assures me that our kids—all four of them—have made their own precious memories right here in our little house, in our little Midwestern town. He is certain that their neighborhood games of tag and baseball, our trips to the zoo and the art museums in a nearby city, are just as precious in their mental scrapbooks as are my memories of an idyllic childhood in the country.

And, you know, he might be right. I think of our oldest son home from college for a visit. He and his brother and sisters sit around the table and reminisce about the good old days—not so very many years ago—when they made a snowman almost ten feet tall in our front yard. They laugh about the water fight that drew almost twenty neighborhood kids into our shady backyard and the wild games of Spoons and Uno we've played around the huge oak table in our kitchen. They fondly remember the walks to our town's arboretum to feed the ducks and turtles and the winter I read *The Wizard of Oz* to the whole family, a chapter every night—or two if they could persuade me.

Life has unfolded in ways we could never predict, let alone plan. That's half the fun. And fortunately, like fine wine, the memories of childhood grow sweeter and more precious with every passing year.

I would imagine that someday Tobi will send her own son or daughter off to college with the same nagging worries. Have I given him all the happy memories I intended him to have? Did I make her childhood as special as she deserved it to be? And the proof—the reassurance—will come unexpectedly, when her own children sit and reminisce about things she didn't plan for a minute . . . things that just happened because life is what happens while we're waiting for the "important" stuff to take place.

Dear Lord, You have created us to live in the now, this very minute. For today is yesterday's hope and tomorrow's foundation. Help me to live today through Your love and under Your guidance and protection. May I be the best parent I can be so that my children's tomorrows will be the best possible future. Amen.

A Pink-Cap and Wedding-Dress Memory

Dee Sanger-Hyatt

Clothe yourselves with compassion,
kindness, humility, gentleness and patience.
Colossians 3:12

Some people think that to make a difference, they must accomplish something spectacular. In truth, the tiniest actions can bring enormous results.

At the time of my wedding, my grandma's health was too poor for her to attend—at least physically. I knew she would be there in spirit. I promised that I would visit her at the nursing home after the wedding, wearing my wedding dress.

As I walked toward my grandma in my wedding dress and veil, her eyes were gleaming from underneath her neon-pink baseball cap, given to her on Mother's Day. We hugged each other and shared tears of joy.

I twirled around, letting her see my dress with the long train. Her eyes danced with pride and love as she fingered the pearled sequins. Grandma and I were floating on cloud nine as we made our way down the hallway. My new husband, Ted, joined our procession.

Everyone asked, "Who are you?"

I proudly held Grandma's hand. "I'm Rena Sanger's granddaughter." Grandma beamed as they congratulated her.

I had transformed a nursing home into a reception without knowing it. I hadn't been prepared for the outpouring of attention but had only wanted to show Grandma my dress.

The residents stood in the hall, cheering and laughing. There was an air of nostalgia, women sighing, maybe reliving their own wedding days.

The dingy hallway was filled with smiling faces and hands reaching out to feel the dress as they wanted to be part of the moment. Even the residents that usually sat with frowns were smiling.

Grandma felt like a queen that day. She was young again, no aches and pains to concern herself with. She sat and enjoyed being a grandma, laughing more than I had seen her laugh for many years.

Grandma is in Heaven now.

My wedding album holds a picture of my proud grandma sitting next to me with her pink cap, me in my wedding dress. We have the same smile, one of love for each other.

Dear Lord, may my memories include wonderful snapshots of special moments and gifts of kindness. A kindness is never wasted, for even if it has no effect on the one to whom it is given, it affects me. For how beautiful will my memories be when they are shaped by kindness. Amen.

The Blanket

D. Harrison

Live a life of love, just as Christ loved us
and gave himself up for us as a fragrant
offering and sacrifice to God.

Ephesians 5:2

I was twenty-three when the news came. Cancer. The doctor said that Mother only had four years to live. It wasn't the news that an only daughter wanted to hear.

It was at this time that I noticed her beginning a sewing project: a blanket. I sensed our time slipping away, and I began to join her in our living room while she worked. I knew from the start how important these times together were for her—and especially for me. There was an urgency in my questions. "Tell me about. . . ." So with each toiled stitch and brilliant color, I learned what made her the woman that she was—her strength, her courage, and her ability to smile in the face of grim situations, even in that of her upcoming death.

As each flower sprouted and blossomed, she shared stories that shaped her life and answered my questions—the childhood farm in Oklahoma, her wedding, Dad's war days, and the birth of each child. I admired her courage and hung on to every word. We chatted about my future. She told me how proud she was that I was going to become a teacher. I made her laugh, and we laughed until our sides hurt. I made sure that she never saw the tears raining inside of me. All the while, I tucked the information into my memory.

Although her hands were plagued with pain, she endured the threading of each needle without complaining. She set her mind to completing the work, as she did with all other tasks. When I complained over mundane tasks, she'd say, "Just be glad that you have the ability to do it." I've carried these words through adulthood.

Each stitch was tiny and perfect, reminding me of her caring, gentle ways. She'd given so much of herself to others—childcare, church work, even in the stitching of this blanket, a labor of perfection to be handed down from mother to daughter. I prayed that I'd glean the lessons she so carefully laid before me: Treat others with kindness, serve God whole-heartedly, and live with the highest standards of integrity. I was so grateful to have a living example of such polished character traits. I vowed to continue within me what was so beautiful in her.

Mother died before the blanket was finished. There was just one block left. Shortly after we laid her to rest my grandmother sewed the last block, a hand-stitched rose. It stands out from the others, made different to symbolize me—different, yet made up of the same things. It is a reminder that we are still a part of each other.

That was twelve years ago and every so often, I unfold the delicate work, careful not to stain it with my tears, wrapping myself in its flowers, comforted in the sweet perfume of her memory—memories made while mother and daughter sat on the couch, sharing their last thoughts, a life coming to an end and a life yet to live.

Dear Lord, how wonderful it is for a mother to give her child a gift that will last—a listening ear and an open heart. May I be a mother who shares this gift with the children You have given me. Amen.

Good News!

Deborah Holt

How good and pleasant it is
when brothers live together in unity!

Psalm 133:1

She didn't plan this third pregnancy; it just kind of happened. Funny how God gives us these surprise gifts, ones we don't immediately recognize as . . . gifts. How was she going to explain this to a three-year-old and a five-year-old who were perfectly content with the way things were and wouldn't relish having to share any of mother's attention with a noisy newcomer?

"You know," she told them one day while they were on one of their walks, "God only picks special boys to be big brothers to a baby sister or brother."

Their innocent voices replied, "He does?"

"Yes," she continued, "maybe you'll be picked one day." She knew it was a setup . . . but maybe not.

Weeks later, when it was becoming more and more difficult to ignore the "abundance of God's generosity" dwelling within her, she told them about a special celebration planned for that evening. There was such excitement and anticipation as she lit some candles and poured sparkling apple juice into the crystal glasses set before them. "Well," she began slowly, "we are celebrating because a wonderful thing is happening . . . Mommy is going to have a baby. That also means that you are going to be big brothers." Her little sons' eyes brightened, and their faces could not hide their delight. She felt relieved and happy but received confirmation that all would be well when her five-year-old looked up at her, candlelight dancing in his innocent blue eyes, and asked, "You mean we're picked?"

Dear Lord, thank You for "picking" me to raise my family. What an incredibly rich gift, one I cannot afford to squander. I realize I do not have enough wisdom to handle this treasure as wisely as I should. Show me how! Amen.

A Tree of Memories

Vickey Banks

I will remember the deeds of the LORD; yes,
I will remember your miracles of long ago.

Psalm 77:11

*C*hristmas was in the air. The sights and sounds
were unmistakable. Tree lots were popping up on
every street corner. Carols were playing on every
radio station. Anticipation bubbled within me as I
looked upon the boxes of decorations my husband
had just brought down from the attic. It was time for
one of my yearly highlights: decorating our family
Christmas tree.

With the enthusiasm of a penniless pirate setting
his eyes upon a long-lost treasure chest, I threw back
the lids and gazed upon my find. Unlike a pirate's
treasure however, it wasn't material wealth I was

seeking. Oh no, it was something far, far more precious to me—memories.

Carefully unwrapping each ornament, I could almost hear it tell me its story. I was taken out of my living room and back in time. The teddy bear sitting in the rocking chair reminded me of the first Christmas I was a mommy. Handling it, I couldn't keep from thinking of how proud my husband and I were as we took picture after picture of our then nine-month-old little girl in her frilly new red Christmas dress—and sent them to virtually everyone we knew!

Some of my favorite ornaments had been gifts from grandparents and a favored aunt who was no longer living. Seeing these, I was reminded of my relatives' love and the times we had shared together. Other ornaments reminded me of treasured friends and trips taken. And, of course, I could see in my mind's eye the proud ear-to-ear grins of my chubby-cheeked children as they had handed me their numerous handmade creations—paper chains, pine cones piled high with glitter, cutout Christmas cards, and various Popsicle-stick compositions.

I knew someone understood why decorating the tree was so meaningful to me when several days later my six-year-old son told me that decorating the tree was his favorite Christmas tradition. When I asked him why, he said, "I like to hear the memories."

Dear Lord, when my children are grown with families of their own, may they hear the memories of long ago. Help them to remember the love and care, the laughter and tears, and the special moments of our lives today. Then, out of the overflow, help them to decorate the lives of their children with precious memories of their own. Amen.

A Mother's Faith

*The faith of a mother can move
any mountain—or at least
tunnel through it.*

Anonymous

Don't Cry, Mommy

Marilyn Mohr

The lions may grow weak and hungry, but those who seek the LORD lack no good thing.

Psalm 34:10

My husband and I had been married for twenty years. We had four lovely children and lived in an upper-middle-class neighborhood. My husband had his own business, and I substituted occasionally in the local schools. We appeared to be a successful family. But underneath the surface, my husband's disease of alcoholism was eating its insidious way to the depths of our marriage. We had tried every possible solution, but nothing worked. Finally, my husband packed up and left.

I found myself on the first day of May, at forty years of age, wondering what would happen next. I had four children to feed. The bills on the desk totaled over $2,200. I had $500 and no job, except for my occasional substitute-teaching work. But now, even that would evaporate as the school district worked on eliminating sixty teaching positions for the coming year. I felt "over the hill" and desperate. There was nothing left to do but turn my situation over to God.

Still, things got worse. Five weeks later, I received seventeen pages of papers filed by my husband asking for a divorce. He asked for everything—and accused me of everything. I felt paralyzed in hopelessness. The children and I needed food and money, and I had nowhere to turn for help.

Less than an hour later, a large car pulled into my driveway. A man, whom I had never seen before and haven't seen since, came to my door. He looked puzzled as he asked, "The Lord Jesus impressed on my wife and me to give food to a family today. I called a friend who suggested this address. Do you need any groceries?"

I couldn't speak, and he nodded with satisfaction and said, "God is always right."

As tears rolled down my cheeks, the man and his wife bustled to and from their car, filling my kitchen with sacks of groceries. After they left, I went to my bedroom and got on my knees to thank God. My five-year-old son found me still sobbing and put his arms around my neck. He said, "Don't cry, Mommy. There's Kool-Aid in those sacks."

Dear Lord, thank You for answering me when I call. You always answer with grace whenever my knees knock with fear. You have taught me that I cannot stumble when I am on my knees. Amen.

Magnified Legacy

Denise Hawkins Camp

I have been reminded of your sincere faith,
which first lived in your grandmother
Lois and in your mother Eunice and,
I am persuaded, now lives in you also.

2 Timothy 1:5

A legacy is a gift that is usually thought of in terms of money, left to families through a will—but not always. My children received a legacy from their grandmother that is far more precious.

Their grandmother, age eighty-four, came to live with us for a short time. Adhering to her morning rituals was the only way she could make it through the day without becoming totally confused. After eating breakfast, Grandmother would take her walker to the den and sit down to do her daily devotion. The problem was, the magnifying glass she needed to read her large-print devotional book was always missing. She used it throughout the day and could never remember where she'd put it.

Every day we searched under chair cushions, beds, and even through the trash. Her walker restricted the number of rooms she could reach, but it was always amazing where we'd find the magnifying glass: the silverware drawer, in a newly folded towel, the medicine cabinet.

Finding Grandmother's magnifying glass became part of my children's morning routine. They even enlisted their friends to help, making it a competitive event.

My son suggested buying another one to eliminate our search. A good idea, but we never could locate the exact brand, and according to Grandmother, nothing else would work. My daughter decided we needed a gigantic glass of our own to aid us in our constant searches.

Even in her sometimes confused state, grandmother realized we were going crazy searching for her glass. She'd tell us, "Don't worry about it," but we would continue looking. For whenever she missed her daily devotion, she'd fret over it the entire day.

This source of frustration became an inspiration to my children. Both remembered the days their grandmother buttoned their clothes and opened jars for them, instead of them doing it for her. Now Grandmother couldn't recall most things from one minute to the next and often asked the same question over and over, but she never forgot to read her Bible.

On days her eyes bothered her, she would ask my second-grader to read the verses. My daughter swelled with pride when her grandmother praised her. My son, after looking at his grandmother's devotional guide, asked if there was one for kids in elementary school.

Four years later, my son is still reading his Bible daily. My daughter still opens her Bible at night and often mentions how good she felt when she read to her grandmother. We still laugh about looking for the magnifying glass, but as we laugh, we grow wistful.

As my mother-in-law's mental and physical health deteriorated, I thought often of her life. She lived through two world wars and the Great Depression.

Her husband had an operation when he was in his mid-thirties that left him handicapped and disfigured. How did she survive it all? Where did she find the strength?

She raised two wonderful sons, was an excellent steward of her finances, and was always willing to help someone in need. Where did she find the guidance?

It didn't take a magnifying glass to find the answer to these questions. One had to look no further than her legacy to her grandchildren.

Dear Lord, if I could choose anything to leave to my children and grandchildren, I would not choose money. I would choose faith, character, and love. For though money can build a house, it takes love to make a home. Amen.

Cheek-to-Cheek

Elizabeth Hey

I have stilled and quieted my soul;
like a weaned child with its mother,
like a weaned child is my soul within me.

Psalm 131:2

Sitting on the edge of my daughter's bed, time slows as we are cradled in soft shadows cast by her mother-bunny night-light. Many nights, after I sing and pray for her, my three-year-old says, "Stay with me."

And so I stay.

Allison reaches up, wraps her arms tightly around my neck, and pulls my face down over hers until my cheek is resting on top of her cheek. Occasionally we talk during our "cheek-to-cheek" time, but most often we are quiet in each other's company.

Silently, she drinks from my presence—security and love, closeness and warmth. Silently, I partake of the wonder of my little girl. How thankful I am that she is able to drink in a love that feeds and nourishes her soul.

I wait until I think she has received her fill before I finally hug and kiss her good night. Often, she is not ready for me to leave. And so we repeat our ritual.

Watching my daughter has given me a childlike picture of myself—a glimpse of what the Lord sees when He looks at me. He views the very essence of who I am without the externals of my daily life. I am reminded, through my daughter and her little-girl simplicity, that the Lord does not define me by my roles as wife, mother, or responsible adult. First and foremost, I am simply His child—His daughter. My Heavenly Father takes delight and joy in me, just as I do in my daughter.

Complete and never-ending love encircles me as I learn to lean into His everlasting arms and draw near to His face. Love and grace flow from His heart into mine. In my Heavenly Father's presence, I find the security I long for as His beloved daughter.

Dear Lord, I am Your daughter. As I rest in Your everlasting arms, I drink in Your love and find security. I want to know You in a more personal way. Thank You for drawing near to me as I draw near to You. You satisfy my longing soul. Amen.

The Small Voice

Linda Evans Shepherd

I trust in you, O LORD;
I say, "You are my God."

Psalm 31:14

One day, I decided to cook a frozen mini-pizza for lunch.

"Can I help?" three-year-old Jimmy asked.

"Get out the cookie sheet and put the pizza on top," I replied.

But when I turned my back to fill our glasses with ice, Jimmy reached for one of my sharp knives and tried to poke a hole in the pizza's cellophane. As he did, the point of the knife skated across the pizza's plastic surface and flew up and into his eye.

As I turned toward him, Jimmy screamed and the knife clattered across the linoleum.

I grabbed at Jimmy as his eyes closed. He fell limp into my arms.

Still cradling Jimmy, I ran to the phone and called our eye doctor. "It's an emergency!" I said. "My three-year-old has poked a knife in his eye! He seems to be unconscious!"

"Bring him in," the receptionist said.

I rushed him to the van.

Why is he so limp? I wondered. *Could the point of the knife have penetrated through his eye and into his brain?*

I intended to drive like a maniac to the doctor's office, but the traffic slowed me down.

I should pray! Eyes opened, I asked, "Lord, did You see what happened? Will Jimmy lose his eye? Did the knife puncture his brain?"

I listened intently.

A still small voice spoke to my heart. *Jimmy is okay.*

Is that You, Lord? I wondered as I pulled into the doctor's office parking lot. My young son was still unconscious, yet I felt a peace as I rushed him inside.

"I can't believe you are so calm," the receptionist said.

After what seemed like hours, the white-coated doctor called us in to see him, and we gently shook Jimmy to arouse him.

Upon carefully examining his eye with fluorescent dye, the doctor finally said, "He got a tiny nick on the edge of his lower eyelid. But he's okay."

"Why did he go limp?" I asked.

"He fainted," Doctor Forrest replied. "Nicks on the eyelid really hurt."

When Jimmy and I left the doctor's office, I felt grateful. Not only was Jimmy okay, but I knew beyond a shadow of a doubt that God's Holy Spirit had really spoken to me. All it took was for me to be willing to ask and to listen for His voice.

Dear Lord, I never have to fear tomorrow, because You are already there. You know my every step. Be a light to my path, so I can keep my life on track. Thank You that I can trust in You. Amen.

Find Me a Doctor

Nancy Bayless

Though I walk in the midst of trouble,
you preserve my life; you stretch out
your hand against the anger of my foes,
with your right hand you save me.

Psalm 138:7

The shrill bell on my telephone jarred me awake. My bedside clock read 11:08 P.M. As I groped for the phone, fear rinsed over me. A strange voice announced with drunken pride, "I've just been in an accident with your son and his motorcycle. He's here at my house. So are the police. He's wiped out his hand. He'll probably lose it. Better come get him—and get a surgeon." He left his address; then his receiver crashed into its holder.

Oh, dear God! Our doctor's in Europe for two weeks. Who else is there in this town? Frantic, I remembered a friend telling me that morning about a doctor who had just moved into the house below ours. I flew to the window and peered down.

Lights gleamed and flames from his fireplace reflected on the windows. I bolted through our front door and out into the frosty night. Asphalt, pebbles, and road film nipped at my bare feet as I raced down the hill through the biting cold, my flannel nightgown tangled around me. *Please, Lord! Don't let Johnny lose his hand!*

Bounding up the stairs to the doctor's house, I pounded on the door, trembling with cold and fear. The door opened. A huge, serious-looking man stood there scrutinizing me. He listened silently to my plea, then took off his jacket and put it on my shoulders.

With slow, deliberate movements he scattered the coals around his fireplace, turned off the living-room light, and led me to his car.

He drove me home, took the jacket from my shoulders and the scribbled address from my hand, and gave me an admonishing nudge toward the front door. "I'll go get him," he said. "Don't worry, I'll take care of him."

I stood frozen to the sidewalk as his car turned around. He stopped and looked at me earnestly. "How old is he?"

"Only twenty-one."

"Good!" he said. "He's a man! Now in the house this minute!"

I didn't salute, but I did move. *A man? My kid? Yes. I guess he is.*

I paced, prayed, and trusted the Great Physician. Logs snapped and popped while I curled up in my favorite chair and opened my Bible. Mark 5:36 NKJV caught my eye. "Do not be afraid; only believe." I believed.

Dawn inched into daylight as they returned. John's hand, encased in bandages and splints, rested in a sling. Stainless-steel staples gleamed on his fingers. He gave me an apologetic smile as he climbed into bed. I tucked the blanket under his chin, while he surrendered with childlike compliance.

The doctor wrote down a few instructions. "Call me day or night if there are any complications. He has a long, painful healing process ahead of him, but only the tip of his little finger and his ring finger will be slightly deformed." He turned to leave.

"I don't even know your name," I said. He handed me his card and turned to walk back toward his house. The sun was just rising.

The tears that I had held back poured down on my face, into my mouth, and drenched the collar of my red, corduroy robe. My daughter, Kathy, dashed into the room, "Mom, what's wrong? Why are you crying so hard?"

I hugged her. "Johnny had an accident. A car hit his motorcycle. I thought he'd lose his hand, but the doctor saved it. He's the new doctor in town. He just moved into the house below us." I wove her fingers around mine as we tiptoed down the hall to look at her brother.

He lay on his back with his mangled hand resting on the pillow. His long eyelashes cast dark shadows across his ashen cheeks.

A kaleidoscope of memories flashed through my mind of nights in the years past when I watched him sleep. In sickness and health, locked away in his own private world of dreams, hopes, and disappointments.

Reaching over to him to turn out his light, I glanced at the doctor's card. Under his name, printed in bold letters, were four words: "Orthopedic Surgeon— Hand Specialist."

My tears spilled out again as I handed the card to Kathy. "You once said you weren't sure if God still creates miracles. He does. Here's one."

Dear Lord, thank You for Your hand in my life. For as Your guide me, You provide for me. You are never more than a prayer away. Thank You for Your loving-kindness. Amen.

Getting Out of God's Way

Barbara Curtis

Hear my cry for mercy as I call to
you for help, as I lift up my hands
toward your Most Holy Place.

Psalm 28:2

Christine's shriek whipped into the room, slicing
my phone call mid-sentence. "Barbara! Hurry! Your
car's rolling down the hill!"

Throwing down the receiver, I spun and raced
down the hall. I could see only the door at the end of
the hall, hear only the pulse surging in my ears as if
something had picked me up, shaken, and booted me
into a more focused dimension.

Seconds slowed and separated like drops from a leaky faucet. I begged, "Oh God, dear God, please let it be empty."

Moments before I had been leaving Christine's office, my toddler in my arms, my oldest son by my side. At the door we had taken extra time for Jonathan to wave bye-bye. When the phone rang, Christine had turned back inside. The parking lot gravel was crunching under my feet when she appeared again at the door to say my husband was on the phone.

"Honey, will you put him in his car seat? I'll be right back," I said to my eleven-year-old son, Joshua, everyone's right-hand man. Christine had asked him to come to physical therapy that day to distract Jonathan from the discomfort and tedium of his workout.

"Sure, Mom," Joshua said. I put his brother into his arms. At three, Jonathan was still too wobbly to negotiate the rocky parking lot safely. Down's Syndrome meant his physical and mental development was delayed. But for his family, his cute little face spelled courage and perseverance. We regarded his features as some would a badge of honor; he had to work so hard for things that came easily to others. Knowing the importance of early intervention for Down's Syndrome children, we had taken Jonathan there weekly since his earliest, floppiest days. You might say we were trying to smooth the road a bit for Jonathan to become all God means for him to be.

Why had my husband called that day? Neither of us remember. He only recalls my cry of dismay and the phone clattering on the floor.

Then my screams, "No! Oh no! Oh, God, please, no!"

The car wasn't empty. Through the windshield, I could see the top of Jonathan's blonde head, framed by his car seat. He was being carried backwards down the sloping driveway toward the two-lane road below. On the other side of the road was a thirty-foot drop into the San Francisco Bay.

As though I were falling down it myself, I felt the agony of what would happen to my little boy in the minute ahead. If the car cleared the roadway without being struck, it would crash down the embankment and end up in the Bay.

"Oh Lord, not here, not now," I pleaded. Moments from Jonathan's brief but difficult life flashed through the memory of my senses. I could hear the beeps of the monitors in the intensive-care unit, see the tangle of cords and wires from the limp body, feel the tug on my stomach when the doctors prepared us for the worst. So many times we had been through these things, with so many people praying for our special little boy. And, one by one, God had healed him of his frailties. For the past year, he had been so healthy we had actually begun to relax.

Would he be stolen from us now, after all God had seen us through?

Not if my son Joshua could help it. Horrified, I saw him behind the car, straining his ninety-five pounds against the ton of metal grinding him backwards. Running awkwardly in reverse as the car picked up speed, he was on the verge of being crushed any second.

I couldn't lose two sons! "Joshua, let go! Get away from the car!" I screamed. Christine was screaming too. Even as we pleaded with him, I understood my son's heart. He always took responsibility.

Everything within him would rage against giving up the battle to save his brother.

I screamed again, "Joshua! Obey me! Let go!"

At last, he jumped away from the car. As Joshua let go, Christine and I stopped screaming. The quiet was eerie. The moment hung poised like the last drop of water from a faucet. The car seemed to hesitate, the rear wheels to shift. Then the car began moving at an angle toward the edge of the driveway, losing momentum, grinding to a halt. Almost gracefully, it came to rest against an old, faithful-looking tree.

Bolting for the car, flinging open the door, I found Jonathan unhurt but bewildered—he never had been in a moving car all by himself before! Catching sight of Joshua right behind me, he grinned and stretched his arms wide—his way of saying, "Life— what an adventure!"

I've been behind a "rolling car" before. I've tried to pit my puny weight against circumstances that were way too big for me to handle. Perhaps that's why I understood Joshua's reaction all too well. "Mom, all I could think of was that I couldn't let him die," Joshua told me later.

I hadn't put my car in park; that little bit of carelessness almost cost me two sons. But thankfully, God intervened and used the situation to teach me a lesson about His mercy and His might. He gave me a picture I will never forget—one son trying to avert disaster, letting go in desperation and being saved. The second son powerless and utterly dependent on God's own outcome.

Because Jonathan is who he is, he might always keep that sweet simplicity. And I will ever be learning from his triumphant trust as he stretches out his arms and smiles, "Life—what an adventure!"

Dear Lord, when I call to You for help, You hear me. I am so grateful. And as I seek Your blessings, help me to seek You. Help me to do what I can, so You can do what I can't. Amen.

A Mother's Courage

*Courage is fear that
has said its prayers.*

Karl Barth

Driving Lessons

Andrea Boeshaar

*Let the morning bring me word of
your unfailing love, for I have put
my trust in you. Show me the way I
should go, for to you I lift up my soul.*

Psalm 143:8

To date, I rejoice that I have lived through two boys learning to drive!

I remember when Ben got his temporary permit three years ago. He asked me if I wanted to take him out driving. Being something of a thrill-seeker, I said, "Okay."

Now I've been to Six Flags Great America, and I have ridden one of its biggest roller coasters with a fifty-foot drop. But even that ride couldn't have prepared me for driving with my son.

"Start putting on your brake, Ben, a stop sign is ahead, a stop sign! Use your brake. YOUR BRAKE!"

As we slammed to a halt, he said, "Not to worry, Mom, I've got everything under control."

My heart thundered in reply.

When Rick started driving, he was the opposite of Ben. He was the overcautious type. I remember once when he took a left turn at a snail's pace. I gasped at the sight of the oncoming traffic headed straight for my side of the car!

"Step on it, Rick!" I cried. "Faster . . . GO FASTER!"

As we made the turn just before the cement truck whizzed by, Rick said, "Not to worry, Mom, I've got everything under control."

I swallowed hard, feeling as though my heart had leapt into my throat.

But the most frightening experience for me occurred when I rode in the backseat. Ben had already earned his regular operator's license by then and was behind the wheel of our '88 black Ford Escort. Rick was sitting in the passenger seat, and Brian, my youngest son, was seated beside me.

"Slow down," I commanded. "You're going too fast."

"Mom, the speed limit is forty and I'm going thirty-five."

"It feels like seventy-five!"

And then I realized it. The most terrifying thing: I had no control. I'd given it up to my son. I was at the mercy of my child who, at the age of eighteen, thought he was invincible. At the age of thirty-eight, I knew I wasn't!

Although, when I was twenty-one and my boys were babies, I guess I might have thought I was invincible too. I would strap them into their car seats, climb behind the steering wheel, and drive away, always confident, always in control—or so I thought. And my babies trusted me. Their shining, young faces would gaze up at me in love, adoration, and even excitement as I buckled them into the car.

I'm beginning to realize that I am no longer in control of my sons' lives. I have handed them the keys and let go. God is the only One who has ultimate control anyway. I can only sit back and try to enjoy the ride.

Dear Lord, give me courage to let go of my children as I hand them the keys to their lives. While they are eager to race into the future, I'm looking for the brakes. Go with them and give me courage to steer through this new phase of our lives. Amen.

The Love Letter

Joyce Simmons

Brothers, I urge you to bear with
my word of exhortation, for I have
written you only a short letter.

Hebrews 13:22

It was a glorious, sun-filled Washington day, and I was determined not to spend it mired in housework. I whisked through the bedroom to pick up the ever present socks that always fell short of the laundry basket. "Must be something in the male genes that makes them unaware that socks don't walk on their own!" I mumbled.

That's when I noticed it. It was on the floor peeking out from the corner of the bed—a pale pink sheet of notepaper carefully folded. In a house full of males, I was unaccustomed to anything pale pink and my curiosity peeked. I quietly turned it over, then slowly unfolded it. I began to read the near perfect handwriting. The apple-blossom scent rose from the paper to match the sweet love poetry written across the page. My knees buckled and my heart raced as I slowly sank to the floor.

How had this happened? How could I be caught so off guard? My mind reflected on all of the faces of women who had told me of similar experiences. I had listened intently and assured them all would be well, meanwhile never thinking it could happen to me.

Perhaps he had been a little distant lately. He had been spending a lot of time away from home. *Just busy,* I determined.

As I held the scented paper against my chest, the tears began to flow. *He is so handsome—so sweet—and he is mine!*

Funny how just the other day I had studied his face as we sat together in church. I noticed he had seemed to change. *Just a little older,* I had mused. *Oh how I love him—how I truly love him.*

The sound of a car door broke through the air. Wiping away the tears, I quickly scurried from the room. *He must not know I'd seen her note—for now it is his secret.* I gathered myself together and headed down the hallway to meet him.

A key in the lock gave me a moment to straighten my hair, dry my face. *He can't see me like this— especially not now!*

The door swung open, golden sunlight flooding into the room around us. There he stood . . . taller than I remembered, and beside him stood a beautiful young lady whose eyes gazed toward the floor as if afraid to meet mine.

"Hi Mom, I'm home," he said, "and there's someone I'd like you to meet!"

Dear Lord, guide my children as they select their dates and mates. Give them wisdom and help them to see beauty is not found just in a pretty face but in goodness and grace. Keep them close to You. Amen.

Laughter

A *family is never poor
when it is rich in laughter.*

Anonymous

The Great Cart Caper

Nancy Kennedy

*He will yet fill your mouth with laughter
and your lips with shouts of joy.*

Job 8:21

My best friend is one. My mom was one. I've always suspected it of my mother-in-law, but she won't tell. In my wildest dreams, I never thought I'd be one, until today.

Today, I joined ranks with millions of women nationwide. Today, I became a two-cart-grocery-shopping mom.

The day began as any other. Cream of rice cereal on the wall. Vaseline smeared on the bathroom mirror. A large purple TV dinosaur and a pajama-clad Barney wannabe singing in the living room.

As I wiped strained apricots off the face of the moving target in the high chair, I noticed my cupboards were bare. I had peanut butter and jelly but no bread. Cereal but no milk. Dirty laundry but no detergent. Dirty hair but no shampoo. If only for clean diapers, I needed to go to the store.

I know this shouldn't have been such a big deal. Women do it all the time, right? Maybe even a man or two has tried it but not me—going to the store with both kids was a whole new adventure.

After baby number two was born, I'd resisted going to the market with both kids, waiting instead to do my shopping when my husband was home. Oh, I've gone shopping with one child. I've even been shopping with both of them, when my husband came too, but never alone with both at the same time. Alone. Unaided by another adult human being.

Did I mention *alone*?

Call me a wimp, but I'd seen two-cart moms before, and their presence intimidated me. With biceps bulging from months (even years) of strenuous pushing and pulling of carts, they'd rove the aisles, their eyes ever moving between bargain fruit cocktail and their two or more securely saddled children. I'd watch from behind the cases of cola, awestruck. Where does a mom go for such training?

Is there a course at the "Y"?

One day I asked my best friend how she learned. "You just do it," she told me.

I asked my mom to go with me. "This is something every woman must do on her own," she said.

Today, I knew it was time.

I loaded the car with supplies: diaper bags, toys, books, infant carrier, backpack, bottles, snacks, and extra clothes. Next came the kids, strapped in the car seats. I flopped into the driver's seat.

"I'm going to do it!" I said and started the car.

Once we arrived at the store, I looked around at the experienced moms to observe proper two-cart procedure: The baby in its infant carrier goes in the back of the cart. The older child sits in the seat, and the other kids go where they fit. Mom goes between the two carts, pushing the cart containing the children and pulling the cart with the groceries.

I positioned the kids in cart number one, took my place, and forged ahead, shoving bagels into one child's mouth and a bottle into the other's, tossing groceries into cart number two. As I huffed and puffed along, I couldn't help noticing the knowing looks from other shoppers. ("Ahh, a novice two-carter.") The word spread throughout the store. ("She's one of us now.")

Encouraging smiles from women between their own carts pushed me onward. "I can do it! I can meet the two-cart challenge! I can win!" I cried.

Into cart number two went cereal, bananas, a box of Huggies, cans of juice. Cart number one— another bagel, another bottle. Pause for a deep breath, then onward. Push, pull, toss the groceries. Push, pull, toss.

Halting the rhythm only for a potty break and a diaper change, I went the distance, crossed the finish line (the checkout counter), and emerged from the market wearing the victor's crown.

I did it!

Chin high, crown firmly in place, I circled the parking lot with my two carts and two kids, looking for my car. Chin a little lower, crown slipping a bit, I circled again. Chin dragging, crown over my eyes, the third go-around revealed my car—and my keys in the ignition. The locked doors leered at me.

A minute before, I was Daniel in the lions' den, Joshua at Jericho, Moses at the Red Sea. I was a two-cart-shopping mom.

Cupping my hands to the windshield for a closer look inside, my victor's crown fell to the ground and shattered at my feet. I had two options: Eat the carton of ice cream before it melted and fall apart, or fall apart and then eat the ice cream. I chose to eat first.

However, in between mouthfuls of mocha almond fudge, I did manage to call the locksmith.

As I sat by my car slurping ice cream, burping one child, entertaining the other, and waiting to be rescued, I reviewed my fleeting moments of victory. I'd faced my greatest fears head-on and won. I pushed myself further than I'd ever imagined. Was the victory worth forty-five minutes in a parking lot with a cartload of spoiling food, tired and cranky children, an ice-cream stomach ache, and a fifty-dollar locksmith bill?

I thought about it long and hard all the way home. I thought about it as I lugged the last bag of groceries into the house and put the kids down for a nap and washed the ice-cream dribbles from my arms. I thought about it as I changed my dirty, sweaty clothes and threw out the previously frozen food that I couldn't refreeze. I thought about it as I put away the rest of the groceries, started dinner, and collapsed on the couch.

I came to this conclusion: Forget facing fears and meeting challenges. Next time, I'll have the groceries delivered.

Dear Lord, it is hard to raise a family. It can be difficult to get them ready to face the world. But I thank You that You walk with me through this journey of motherhood, from the grocery store far into the distant future. Amen.

Three Red Dresses

Golden Keyes Parsons

Sarah said, "God has brought me laughter, and everyone who hears about this will laugh with me."

Genesis 21:6

Thanksgiving days had always found the Parsons' household filled with the mingled fragrances of cinnamon, sage, onions, celery, buttermilk, and pumpkin pies. As our three daughters grew older and developed their own personal favorites, I found myself having to make one of each favorite dish, making the Thanksgiving menu a rather large one.

That particular year, our oldest daughter had three children—a two-year-old, a three-year-old, and an infant. Our middle girl was a sophomore in college and the youngest a senior in high school.

I struggled that year to make the holidays festive. My husband and I had been involved in a wonderful conference ministry the ten years previous, but the center sold, and we had been let go. In the transition we had to leave our home as well as our ministry. It was the beginning of the second holiday season since our unceremonious dismissal. We had moved twice. We had not found profitable employment, and our oldest daughter and her husband were separated.

As the crisp days of autumn began to draw toward Thanksgiving, our family had a major problem fulfilling some of its traditions . . . one in particular. In our little rented house, we had no cook stove. I had an electric skillet and a microwave but no oven in which to cook the traditional turkey. After our oldest daughter and her husband separated, she and her babies moved into a small house across the street. She did have a cook stove. We decided that we would cook the turkey and dressing in her oven and bring it over in time for the Thanksgiving dinner. We baked the pies at her house, as well, going between the two houses all day preparing, as best we could, a sumptuous Thanksgiving feast. The two oldest grandchildren ran back and forth, squealing with delight over the festivities.

"Papa, watch!" they cried as they swung on the tire swing in the front yard. They played in the leaves in the yard, oblivious to our frustration at providing a warm, memorable holiday for them. There was plenty of love, kisses, and hugs to go around, even though the wounds of separation of a marriage and the loss of a home and a career were still raw and tender.

One of the traditions upon which I had insisted was dressing up for holiday dinners—until the girls got old enough to make their own decisions! When they were little, I usually had them outfitted in matching dresses with tights and their blonde hair done up in bows and frills. Once, when the girls and I were all dressed up in our "Sunday best" and the table was beautifully set with china and silver, my husband came to the table dressed in jeans and a T-shirt—complete with a tie! All sense of decorum was lost for the evening under gales of hysterical laughter. As the girls grew older, they began to resist and wanted to wear jeans or shorts. I held out as long as I could, but I had given it up years before. Actually, it was not that big of a deal. We loved each other, we were healthy, and we were together. There was an abundance of God's provision for which to be grateful. I barely gave it a passing thought that year.

The time was approaching to go get the turkey. The girls and grandchildren stayed at our house, preparing the table, filling the glasses—munching on goodies as they worked. My husband and I went across the street to bring the turkey over. As I went out the door, I casually mentioned over my shoulder, "I suppose it wouldn't do any good to ask you girls to dress up, would it?" The girls looked at me and rolled their eyes.

We basted the turkey a bit more and stayed longer than we had anticipated, letting the dressing brown up nicely. We walked across the street, carefully balancing our Thanksgiving Tom on a tray, with steam rising from the dressing in the cool air of that fall afternoon in East Texas. As we opened the door of our house, there stood our three beautiful grown daughters in red evening gowns—laughing and giggling as they had done when they were little towheaded girls.

As soon as my husband and I left to go across the street to get the turkey, they had raced to the youngest daughter's closet and gotten her junior prom dress which was red, the red formal gown she was wearing that year as the senior girl representing our small town, and the red gown that our daughter in college wore as a nominee for college beauty. There they stood—arm in arm—laughing as we came in.

"Is this dressy enough for you, Mom?"

My husband and I laughed and cried as we all hugged and then turned to celebrate a memorable Thanksgiving dinner. We look back on that Thanksgiving with fondness. Even at one of the lowest points in our lives, the spirit of love God had showered on our family triumphed over the difficult circumstances and pointed us toward what is truly important . . . love, acceptance, laughter, and family unity.

Dear Lord, the best holiday gift is the presence of a happy family, wrapped in love. Please help my family to be able to exchange this gift with one another. Teach us how to enjoy each other and to love, accept, and laugh together in unity. Amen.

Do You Know Me?

Nancy Kennedy

*Be shepherds of God's flock that is
under your care, serving as overseers—
not because you must, but because you
are willing, as God wants you to be;
not greedy for money, but eager to serve.*

1 Peter 5:2

There's a container of neon-pink Silly Slime dumped in the bottom of my purse and a half-eaten, squished, strawberry Pop Tart in my jacket pocket. I wear baggy sweats with elastic waists. I know every Raffi song by heart. I live for nap time. My heart pounds for Mr. Rogers—he likes me just the way I am.

I wash my children's faces with spit and my thumb. Pick at the dirt behind their ears. Show their rashes to anyone who'll look. Wipe their noses with my shirt.

123

I'm sure you've seen me at the market. I'm the one with the permanent stain on my shoulder from baby spit up, the one with dirty footprints on my shirt from the nonstop kicking of my child sitting in the grocery cart. The one who didn't have an answer to the loudly asked question, "Do we have to eat dog food again tonight?"

You've probably seen me at the mall trying to maneuver a stroller with a crying baby who's struggling to get out, while chasing another child who can be twelve places at once. I'm the one carrying the worn-out blankie and Cabbage Patch doll that I warned I wouldn't carry. The one shouting: "Don't touch! I said, DON'T TOUCH!" The one muttering, "I'm never doing this again."

You know who I am. I'm the one with the glazed look on my face after answering for the millionth time, "I don't know what worms eat." I consider myself lucky to get a shower by noon.

I eat leftover baby food smeared on toast for breakfast. I drink leftover milk with graham cracker crumbs floating in it. I eat the crusts nobody wants.

You know me. I'm bleary-eyed from being up all night with a teething baby and teary-eyed from worrying about a toddler who refuses to eat. I have baby drool and oatmeal in my hair. I can't remember the last time I had a whole night's sleep or a hot cup of coffee. The only book I've read in the past six months is *Good Night Moon*.

I never get to finish a senten—

I love my husband but (yawn) . . . ZZZZZ.

I used to be reasonably intelligent, pondering the deep secrets of the universe. Now I find myself wondering such things as: If Bert and Ernie aren't related, why do they sleep in the same room? And where are their parents?

I remember a time when getting together with friends meant stimulating conversations about current events, about love and the meaning of life. Now we talk for hours about which is better—cloth or disposable? Pacifiers or thumbs? Know any good potty-training tips?

Maybe you've seen me at church. I'm the one with my skirt on backwards or the entire inner facing of my dress hanging out. In my rush to get everybody else dressed, I often forget to check my own appearance.

I know you didn't know my first name—I don't have one anymore. I answer to any child calling, "Mom, Mommy, Mama, and WAAAAAHHH!"

To be honest, I don't even remember my first name—I've stopped using it myself. When speaking, I simply refer to myself as "Mommy."

"Mommy says to stop pulling the cat's ears."

"Mommy's ears can't hear whining."

"Yes, Mommy's wearing her angry face."

"Do you want Mommy to use the spanking spoon?"

I have my good days, days when we get through breakfast without oatmeal on the wall, days when the cat doesn't end up in the toilet, days when everyone takes a nap at the same time.

On those days, I feel powerful—in control. I can nurse a baby and cook dinner at the same time. I can even nurse a baby and talk on the phone and fold laundry and watch Oprah all at the same time.

You know who I am.

I am Mommy. And I don't even need an American Express Card to prove it.

Dear Lord, I am Mommy. Help me to feed, love, and clothe my little lambs. Show me how to shepherd them away from the pitfalls of life. Help me to lead my flock to cool waters, lush meadows, and wisdom. Help me to mother with love. Amen.

Surprised by Motherhood

DiAnn Mills

Our mouths were filled with laughter, our
tongues with songs of joy. Then it was
said among the nations, "The LORD
has done great things for them."

Psalm 126:2

My life has been an adventure since the birth of my six children. All six are extremely curious and active. Life holds new surprises every day. I selected to home-school all of them, so I have been privileged to see every aspect of their lives as a mother and as a teacher.

Some of the things I've experienced I wish I hadn't, but such is raising children. One of the latest escapades at our house involved my three youngest

children. It had been raining for days; but when the sun peeked through, I seized the opportunity for Benjamin, age eight, Angela, age six, and Andrew, age three, to play outside. Naturally, I made it quite clear that they all were to stay away from the mud.

I busied myself inside, attempting to get a few things done around the house. The solitude felt wonderful until Benjamin came running into the house, breathless with a look of panic spread across his face.

"Andrew is stuck in the mud!" he cried.

"What is he doing in the mud?" I demanded.

I followed Benjamin outside. *He knows better than this,* I fumed. I could feel the anger race through my body. Couldn't I have one moment of peace?

Andrew was easy to spot since he stood waist deep in a mud hole.

"I told you to stay out of there," I said firmly. I noticed that my two older children were also covered from head to toe in mud. Right then I decided to bring them all in for a bath. It would probably take until supper to get them clean.

My first thought was to pull Andrew from the hole. I reached behind him and grabbed him securely underneath his arms. I attempted to lift him, but he wouldn't budge! *Hmm,* I thought, not the least bit discouraged. *I'll try something different.* This time I stepped in front of him, straddled the hole, and lifted again. Nothing moved; Andrew was stuck. The more I pulled on him, the more he hollered.

"You're hurting me. You're hurting me!" he shouted for the entire neighborhood to hear.

"I know, honey, but I've got to get you out of there," I replied. The last thing I needed was a hysterical three-year-old.

Determined to free him from the mud, I yanked again. Andrew continued to protest against my futile attempts at rescuing him until my ears rang. I begged him to stop wailing, especially since the neighbors probably thought I was beating him.

Then the realization crept all over me. The mud around his waist had set at his feet, anchoring Andrew solidly in the hole.

Andrew struggled and screamed, and I sensed that his former prank now frightened him. From seemingly nowhere a man appeared. His sudden intrusion into my predicament startled me.

"Can I help you?" he asked. "Looks like the little guy is stuck tight."

I didn't know him, and I felt hesitant to accept his help, but what could I do?

"Well, okay, I certainly don't know how to get him out," I replied and quickly explained what had happened.

"Got a shovel?" he asked, and I sent Benjamin off to the garage.

The man dug around Andrew's body to determine the angle at which he had slipped into the hole. He leaned on the shovel and studied his work.

"Try standing behind him again," he finally said. "Take a much wider stance and pull hard."

I took a deep breath and did exactly as he suggested. Not an ounce of movement came from Andrew's body. He screamed again and tried to twist his little body free. I tried to calm him down, but he wanted out—right then.

"I'm sorry," I moaned, to the man. "This really isn't your problem."

"Oh, we'll get him out," he assured me. He plunged his hand down into the mud up to his armpit and found one of Andrew's shoes. Once he loosened it, he began pulling up. I could not believe the struggle just to lift my son's foot. At last Andrew's knee showed near the surface of the mud. Feeling quite victorious, I reached behind him to yank him up, but the other foot was still stuck so tightly that Andrew couldn't budge. I knew his arms ached from me lifting him, but I kept thinking one more burst of energy would set him free.

The man and I dug out mud from behind Andrew's knees until the other foot loosened. At last, I pulled Andrew completely out. I handed my son to the man who deposited him on the grass nearby. The man offered his hand to assist me, and you guessed it. I was now stuck in the mud surrounding the hole!

I saw humor in it, but oh, I felt embarrassed. I still had no idea of the man's identity, and, looking around, I didn't see a car either. After he successfully helped me from the mud, he introduced himself as the son of a couple from across the street. I thanked him profusely and encouraged Andrew to do the same.

"Raising kids must be really difficult," he commented.

"Yes," I replied. "It's always full of surprises."

As the man walked back to his parents' home, I could hear him laughing. I guess we did look like quite a sight.

In repeating the story to my husband, the whole thing became incredibly funny, and I'm sure the man who helped us will never forget his vivid encounter with the surprises of motherhood.

Dear Lord, I am always surprised by being a mom. It is full of pitfalls and mud holes. As my children splash through life, may I be there not only to dry their clothes but to dry their tears. Help my darling, daredevil children turn into decent, delightful adults. Amen.

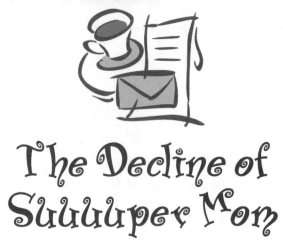

The Decline of Suuuuuper Mom

Carla Edmisten

"You are worried and upset about many things, but only one thing is needed."

Luke 10:41-42

"How lazy can you be?" I asked my dear friend Carrie when she proudly announced that she had just ordered pizza because she was out of diet soda and didn't feel like making the trip to the grocery store. What a wonderful discovery. "They'll actually bring a six pack right to my door. If only they had Pop-Tarts, this would be a perfect world." Embarrassed for her, I smugly held on to my title of "Suuuuuper Mom." She had bestowed this upon me with an inflection of sarcasm as only a best friend can. And I translated it, as only a best friend can, "You're just jealous because preparing a balanced meal to you is asking for a tomato slice with the kid's meal, and your answer to housekeeping is not answering your door."

"Can you say N-O?" she always responds when I make the mistake of reciting my litany of to-dos to her. And perhaps she has a point. Just like the Wednesday night when I found myself at church with a broken toe, two small children, and a husband out of town. Of course these minor inconveniences were not going to keep me at home. Risk that someone might think I can't handle everything? Someone might think less of me? Worse yet, might I think less of myself? Never!

But that's when it started, the beginning of the end. As the pastor's message neared the close, my mind was fixed on the dread of getting the kids in and out of the car one more time and hobbling, broken-toed, in the cold into the grocery store. There must be an easier way. I scolded myself: Why hadn't I planned better? A truly efficient, well-organized homemaker would, at the very least, have a supply of powdered milk on hand. *If only we didn't live in such a rural area, I, too, could have pizza delivered, and hey, they just might bring me some milk too. How did that poison slip into my consciousness?* "I cannot become Carrie, I cannot become Carrie." I began the chant. I hurried from the sanctuary and gathered my children, avoiding eye contact with everyone.

A cold sweat running down my back and paranoia building, I could almost hear them saying, "Look, she has no milk at home, and she's actually considering how she could have some delivered." Next they will be shaking their heads with disapproval and saying, "Those poor children."

If only I could make it to the car, I could slap myself back into reality, wash my face with a cold baby wipe—I would once again be convinced that there was only one way out. Do the right thing . . . boldly march into the grocery store.

The chanting grew fainter, "I will not become . . ." *How did I get here?* I should have gained control and sped away. Perhaps the exhaust fumes billowing in my window had rendered me powerless. After a long pause, the muffled voice blared through the menu board, "Do you want fries with those six milks?"

Dear Lord, help me to use the experience I've acquired to become a better mom. Help me to pass on the wealth of my experience to my kids, for my best advice may come from my worst mistakes. Help me to train my children in the way I should go myself. Amen.

What Superglue Joins Together, Let No One Put Asunder

Rhonda Wheeler Stock

I will forget my complaint, I will change my expression, and smile.

Job 9:27

"Would you care to explain what happened?" I asked.

"We-e-l-l-l," began Josh, the thirteen-year-old, "we didn't mean to break it."

"M-m-m." I picked up a tiny fragment of porcelain and tried to figure out if it was part of the bride's veil or the groom's right foot.

"It didn't break the first time it fell," offered eleven-year-old Jason helpfully.

"The first time?" I was trying hard not to scream, at least not until I had the full story. Then the yelling could commence.

"Yeah." Jason realized he had made a tactical error. "See, it fell off the wall and . . ."

"It fell off the wall?"

"Actually, it was the shelf," said Josh.

"The shelf?"

"Yeah. The shelf it was sitting on fell off the wall, so it fell down too," said Jason.

"Go on," I sighed.

"We put the shelf back up and put the figurine on it," said Josh.

"And then?" I prodded.

"Then we knocked it off the shelf." Jason shifted uncomfortably.

I tapped a finger against the box which contained the remnants of the happy porcelain couple. "And that's when it broke."

The boys nodded.

"We couldn't fix it," added Jason, "so we put it in that box."

The three of us stared silently into the box. Finally, I said, "Your father gave me this figurine as an engagement present. It was the first piece in my collection—for a long time it was the only piece in my collection. It's been around all these years, even with all our moves and everything." My restraint started to slip. "And now it's broken. I've had this for sixteen years! I've had it longer than I've had you!"

I didn't know whether to scowl or weep. Jason looked properly solemn, but Joshua's mouth was twitching suspiciously. "Well," he said, struggling to contain his grin, "now you have it in sixteen pieces."

Jason's eyes widened in shock. I'm sure mine glowed red.

"Joshua . . ." Then I made my fatal mistake: I looked into his eyes. And I laughed. I couldn't help it;

Joshua's wisecrack was just short of disrespectful, but it was also clever and, well, funny.

When I stopped giggling, I sent them outside with the promise that they would be disciplined as soon as I decided what was appropriate (assuming that grounding them for life was illegal in my state).

I looked into the box and stirred the fragments with my finger. I was pretty sure my husband could glue the pieces back together. He has a knack for that sort of thing, which is one of the reasons I love him. And I realized that a broken figurine could always be replaced, unlike a broken marriage or a broken heart. The boys would certainly be disciplined, not so much because I was upset over the shattered bride and groom but because they needed to learn to respect other people's property, to behave in a civilized manner, and not to cover up their sins.

But I wouldn't ground them for life. Oh no. Because then I'd have to support them for the next seventy or eighty years. And that would make me scream.

Dear Lord, sometimes raising kids gets a bit emotional. Help me know when it's okay to laugh and when it's okay to cry. For both laughter and tears are required when it comes to being a parent. Amen.

A Mother's Heart

*Children leave indelible
imprints on a mother's heart.*

Anonymous

Kissed by an Angel

Judy L. Dudley

*We were gentle among you, like a
mother caring for her little children.*

1 Thessalonians 2:7

I have just been kissed by an angel. Actually, I have
been kissed by four angels, but there is one in
particular I would like to tell you about. She is three
years old, wears a ponytail on the top of her head
(which makes her look like Pebbles Flintstone), and
she is usually full of so much joy you can't help but
smile when you're around her. She just came into my
bedroom to give me a goodnight kiss, her oversized
T-shirt dragging on the floor, and her beautiful eyes
sparkling with love for Mommy. She climbed up on
my bed and, wrapping her little arms around my
neck, she pressed her sweet lips to my cheek and told
me she loved me.

Ah, can life get any better than this? I truly can't imagine what my world would be like without this heavenly gift. Sure, she is frustrating at times, like the time she hit her little brother because he had something she wanted or when she wrote on her bedroom wall with a permanent marker. Yet I believe God knew exactly what He was doing when He placed Laura in our lives. He knew I needed something different after giving me first a strong-willed child, then a quiet, submissive one. Laura puts the "bounce" into our predictable days. I never know what she will do next. She is like an unexpected, refreshing rain shower in the midst of a hot summer's day. She is the cream in my coffee, the cherry on my sundae, and the icing on my cake. My life would not be complete without her.

About a month ago, on Mother's Day, Laura brought home a gift for me, something she made in Sunday school. It was a flower made from her handprint. I remember thinking how her hand would not be this size for long, so I was thrilled to receive a permanent reminder of it.

You see, this small hand also holds my heart. It has such a grip on me at times that it hurts, but it is a pain I pray will never go away. It is the grip of love that lasts a lifetime. But Laura will not be three years old forever. So, as the days go by and my little girl grows, I will continue to thank God for sending her to us and for giving me the cherished memories of days of sunshine smiles, flower handprints, and angel kisses.

Dear Lord, my children will not be young forever. Help me to cherish all the moments of both sunshine and rain. For joy comes in the tiny moments of life. Help me to imprint them upon my heart. Thank You for all the moments of joy. Amen.

Right Where I Want to Be

Wendy Dunham

He settles the barren woman in her home as a happy mother of children. Praise the LORD.

Psalm 113:9

Forget the movies and fine dining on a Saturday night—I was home and having fun. My daughter, Erin, had just transformed our bathroom into a beauty parlor and could hardly wait to begin my makeover.

I watched Erin as she strategically arranged her "makeup" and Barbie cologne on our vanity. She had chosen deep orchid lipstick (purple), peony nail polish (neon pink), lavender eye shadow (with sparkles), and mid-pink blush, ("bubble-gum flash" might have done it more justice).

As she lavishly applied the purple lipstick, she said, "Mom, you look so great!" Then with all her six-year-old sincerity, she looked at me like I was the most beautiful woman in the world. And for those few moments, I believed I was.

With her tiny comb, she "fixed" my hair so it was flat against my head and placed her plastic pearls around my neck. "Wait here, Mom," she said, "I'll be right back." She soon returned with earrings. "I've picked just the right ones," she assured me and displayed my jingle-bell earrings in her palm. Being six, she didn't care that Christmas was already four months past.

Next she brought in my wedding shoes; it had been eleven years since I'd stepped into them. As she slipped them onto my feet, I was Cinderella at last. It wasn't long, however, before my feet were numb and my toes tingled; ankle socks and fallen arches left little room for comfort. But I kept them on, for we hadn't yet had our dance.

For her finishing touch, Erin tied two scarves together for a shawl and placed them around my shoulders. "There, Mom," she said, "you're gorgeous!"

We had our dance, and that night I was the most beautiful (and the most blessed) mom in the whole world. My grown-up soul had been restored with the joy, hope, and wonder of a child. And as we waltzed through our living room, I couldn't help but think, "This is right where I want to be."

Dear Lord, teach me to hear the music as I waltz with my children. May my lead be worth following. Thank You for teaching me the dance and for giving me such wonderful partners. Amen.

Forty and...

Judith A. Wiegman

The righteous will flourish like a palm tree,
they will grow like a cedar of Lebanon;
planted in the house of the LORD, they will
flourish in the courts of our God. They
will still bear fruit in old age, they will
stay fresh and green, proclaiming,
"The LORD is upright; he is my Rock,
and there is no wickedness in him."

Psalm 92:12-15

The doorbell rang. There stood my friend Ruth. "Come on," she began, "let's go to Amarillo. It will do you good. We can have a nice lunch and shop. I brought Carrie—she can stay here with your children."

Reluctantly, I accepted her offer. I wasn't sure I would be good company, but I really did need the diversion. Ruth knew; she always knew.

The west-Texas panhandle is picturesque and calming. The majestic canyons, wildlife, and awesome cloud formations reflect God's handiwork. Crest a certain hill and you will see, sprawling below like a sleeping giant, Amarillo. It looks out of place amidst the prairie grass and canyon decor. The trip was worth it. I was refreshed.

We shopped, laughed, had a great lunch, and decided to check out one more store before heading home. We ended up in the card section.

Ruth heard a weeping sound coming from my direction. She rounded the corner with a salesclerk. They found me, leaning against the counter, arm outstretched, pointed to something, sobbing loudly.

Ruth probably wanted to burst out laughing, but she knew better. There I stood, eyes fixed on a barbecue apron that adorned the wall. It carried this message: "I'd rather be 40 than pregnant." I was both.

We left the store and headed home. In the car I silently recalled the events that had brought me to that moment. My previous pregnancy, number six, had been difficult. Plagued with kidney infections during the nine months, I underwent surgery for kidney stones shortly after the baby was born.

I remember phrases from a conversation between the doctor and my husband as I drifted in and out after the surgery. He cautioned that another pregnancy could put my life in great danger. The decision was made, and my husband agreed to a vasectomy.

Over a year later, I began experiencing "flu-like" symptoms every morning. I knew I was pregnant. No one would listen, but I knew.

One morning after the five older children left for school, I walked to the drugstore and purchased a pregnancy test. It was positive. I cried for most of the day. Even a vasectomy, the ultimate step, had failed.

I wrapped a tiny pair of yellow booties and placed them on my husband's pillow. That night in the quiet darkness, we each had to deal with the obvious. He chose acceptance. I chose bitterness.

On a hot sticky day in July, in my sixth month of pregnancy, I was shaken from that bitterness. I heard my son and husband talking as they came in and washed up for supper.

"Who's going to tell her?" my son questioned.

"Let's wait and see how she is," was the reply from my husband.

"Tell me what?" I queried as I walked into the room. They just stood there, water dripping from their hands.

The story spilled out. Connie, my pregnant friend whose baby was due in two weeks, had been taken to Amarillo. Her baby had died and had been taken by C-section.

A few days later, standing beside a tiny white casket in the scorching Texas sun, my thoughts were of Connie, still in the hospital. She had stood here before, after tragedy struck, and buried her first son. How thrilled she was to carry this child, hoping for a son to add to her beautiful family of three precious girls.

We laid to rest her second son, Martin Richard James III. I left the cemetery with a struggle raging and my live child kicking inside.

Later that afternoon, I drove to the edge of town and parked by the lake. I kicked off my sandals and walked along the shoreline. Reaching down, I cradled my unborn child sleeping inside. Reality struck! I wasn't walking alone. Every step and every breath I took belonged to the two of us. I began to weep. I accepted my pregnancy and my child as a gift from God. I had forgotten how He had brought me through the six months of pregnancy up to that point without a serious medical problem. I sought my baby's forgiveness and His. I bonded to my unborn child, and there was joy.

Knowing it would be hard, I went to see Connie when she came home. She was gracious. She instructed me not to hide from her for the next three months and assured me of her happiness for me. We wept together. In her time of grief, she blessed me.

In the October of my childbearing years, in the month of October, my little girl arrived. I brought home our unexpected blessing to six delighted siblings, ranging in age from seventeen to two.

Connie came to the house. Instinctively I placed my pink bundle in her arms. And true to her name, Autumn Joy brought joy, unmistakable joy.

Dear Lord, You bless me in unexpected ways—and in "expecting ways." I may not have expected this child You have given me, but she was not a surprise to You. For You have planned on her arrival before the beginning of this age. May I forever be like an expectant mother, pregnant with hope and trust in You. Amen.

Undercover Cat

Donna McDonnall

*Judge nothing before the appointed time;
wait till the Lord comes. He will bring to
light what is hidden in darkness and will
expose the motives of men's hearts. At that
time each will receive his praise from God.*

1 Corinthians 4:5

It had been a long, nerve-racking week of isolation at the hospital. Our son Danny had been running a fever after receiving chemotherapy for bone cancer. During that time, his white-blood-cell count was dangerously low.

Any signs of infection, such as a fever, had to be treated as an emergency.

His blood count would get better; it was just a matter of time.

Meanwhile, long tedious hours passed slowly as we waited in his "isolation" room at the hospital. No one could enter his room without putting on special hospital gowns, gloves, caps, masks, and booties.

Visitors were limited to the immediate family. Danny, his older brother, David, and I were making rather feeble attempts to pass the time by playing board games. Frankly, we were quickly becoming edgy and bored with each other.

"Mom, could David bring my cat over and hold it up outside my window, just so I could see it?" Danny asked.

"Well, I guess that wouldn't hurt anything," I agreed.

David went home and shortly returned with Tig. Danny seemed to come to life when David held Tig up outside Danny's ground-floor window.

"Mom, open the window just so I can pet him."

The screenless window was built low to the floor. It seemed a simple thing to do and was obviously helping to cheer up Danny.

OK," I conceded.

Danny's window was opened. Danny stretched out his hand and immediately a broad smile broke across his face as his fingers stroked the soft fur. Tig was also enjoying the moment as he stretched, purred, and rubbed against Danny's hand.

"Mom, couldn't I bring him into my room and hold him just for a few moments?" Danny coaxed. "I'll be careful. The nurses will never know."

Suddenly the decisions were becoming more complicated. Normally, a very conservative, "stick-to-the rules" type of mother, I was also a nurse who had worked at that hospital. This was obviously not standard, or even acceptable, behavior. Yet, there stood my son, fighting a life-threatening illness, asking for what seemed like a fairly simple request that would bring him much pleasure.

Trying to rationalize my decision with medical-sounding judgment, I replied. "O.K., just this once. It will probably boost your immune system by bringing you happiness."

After passing the cat through the window, David came around to the hospital's front entrance and after going through the elaborate isolation dressing procedure, entered Danny's hospital room. We had decided the cat could stay for thirty minutes and then would be returned home. We did not expect any hospital personnel to come for at least another hour.

No sooner had we all become engrossed in petting and playing with Tig when we heard the nurse outside Danny's room preparing to enter.

"Here, stick Tig under your isolation gown, David. She'll never see him," Danny instructed as he quickly passed Tig to David.

As David futilely tried to stuff the cat under the gown, the nurse began to open the door to Danny's room. Realizing, the "stuffing" method wasn't going to work, David dashed into the bathroom, locking himself and the now very confused cat inside.

As fate would have it, the nurse had entered to complete a rather time-consuming procedure. She was so engrossed in her work that she apparently did not notice the faint meowing sounds.

Finishing her task, she turned to enter the bathroom to wash her hands. Just as she was reaching for the doorknob, Danny shouted, "Don't go in, my brother is in there!" at which point, I heard scratching at the door and David trying to make "cover-up" sounds such as coughing and flushing the toilet. There seemed to be a lot of commotion going on in the bathroom.

The nurse politely tried not to notice and pleasantly chatted with Danny, waiting for David to exit the bathroom so she could wash her hands.

After what seemed an inordinately extended time, David came out of the bathroom wearing a very rumpled and lumpy gown. Quickly plopping onto Danny's bed, he tried to covertly keep the cat covered.

Just as the nurse turned to leave, the cat had had enough undercover work. With a bound, he leaped out from under the gown and sheets, landing uncere-moniously at the feet of one very surprised nurse.

"Well, hello there!" She greeted Tig. "Did you come to visit Danny today?"

Chagrined, I apologized, "We thought it would cheer Danny up if we brought his cat in. I'm sorry if we caused trouble."

Being a true caregiver, the nurse graciously replied, "No problem. We welcome all members of the patient's family." With that she turned and left the room, never mentioning the incident again.

The week passed very quickly after that, and Danny's blood count rose to a near-normal level rapidly.

Dear Lord, there is nothing hidden from You. For that I am grateful. I give everything I am and have to You because You can do a lot more with my life than I can. Thank You for shedding the light of Your truth and love into the darkness. Amen.

Next to My Heart

B o n n i e   C o m p t o n   H a n s o n

From birth I have relied on you;
you brought me forth from my
mother's womb. I will ever praise you.

Psalm 71:6

The day I had to stop dead in my tracks in the aisle of a busy supermarket was one of the worst in my whole life.

There I was, pregnant as could be—forty pounds overweight, a whole month past my due date with wretched "morning sickness" that lasted twenty-four hours every single day. And now I had charley horses in both feet, so excruciating I couldn't move.

This wasn't the way I had expected pregnancy to be. My own mother, who had six children, glowed when she was expecting. Her mother, my grandmother, not only joyfully welcomed sixteen little ones into the world—but ran a busy store the entire time. Looking forward to holding a little one, they said, and feeling the miracle of life inside should make any woman ecstatically happy—and healthy!

In all my magazines, the maternity advertisements showed blissful mothers-to-be in adorable outfits, perfect hairdos—even high heels. And that's the way my expecting friends were. A coworker with the same due date as mine worked right up to the time her baby came. My next-door neighbor had done everything she wanted to for nine full months (while looking absolutely gorgeous). Neither had been ill a minute. And both of them now had adorable, healthy babies.

Meanwhile, I was still pregnant, still miserable, and so large I had long since forgotten what either my feet or my legs looked like. There was only one outfit I could even fit into—a sort of muumuu tent. I'd had to give up work and involvement at church—and I almost gave up hope.

Why was God allowing this to happen to me? He knew I loved Him, my husband, and this unborn child. My friends had started snickering: "You were due when?" Even my doctor grumped at me as if it were my own fault.

And now during one of the hottest Augusts on record, my ankles swelled so badly in our sweltering apartment, I had to keep them in buckets of ice.

Going anywhere was torture. But we were out of milk. Just a quick dash to the store, I thought—surely I could do that.

So there I was, frozen in my tracks, stopping carts in both directions.

My face beet red, I stared at the rows of cracker boxes in front of me—pretending not to notice the angry shoppers whose way I was blocking.

And then I heard a little girl's voice: "Mommy, why does that lady look so funny?"

I squeezed my eyes shut, trying to stop sudden tears. *Oh, God, please!*

That's the last straw! Can't anyone say anything nice about me for a change? Won't I ever be normal and comfortable and well again? Won't I ever get to hold this baby in my arms?

Then that mother said something I will never forget. "Dear," she said softly, "it's because God has given that woman a tiny baby to carry next to her heart."

When I opened my eyes, mother and daughter were gone. Eventually, so were the charley horses. But those words have lasted a lifetime.

For, oh, they are so true. They were such a blessing to me during those final miserable days before I did hold my beautiful firstborn in my arms as well as during my next two pregnancies. A blessing I remembered as my three children grew up and married. A blessing I have been privileged to share with my own pregnant daughters-in-law and many other young women I have known over the years.

For even after our children are born, we mothers carry those precious little ones next to our hearts, even when they are grown up and have children of their own—and we will our whole lives long.

Dear Lord, thank You for the children You have placed in my heart. Help me to love and cherish them so I can bring them up—and not let them down. Keep me strong so that I never give in when I shouldn't or give up when the going gets tough. Amen.

Teaching Moments

Judicious mothers will always keep in mind, that they are the first book read, and the last put aside, in every child's history.

C. Lenox Remond

Pillow Fright

Deborah Raney

"In your anger do not sin": Do not let the sun go down while you are still angry.

Ephesians 4:26

*O*ur oldest daughter, Tobi, is our strong-willed child. We recognized her independent spirit and her stubborn will almost from the day she was born. While we were living through the challenges of raising a spirited little girl like Tobi, it wasn't always easy to see the humor in things. Fortunately, hindsight has allowed us to see many of those struggles in a different light.

One afternoon, when Tobi was at the height of her fiery preadolescent years, she became furious with me because I wouldn't grant her permission to do something. (Of course, neither of us can even remember what it was now!) At any rate, she started "acting out" physically. As she slammed doors and slapped books loudly onto the table, I did my best to keep my cool.

"Tobi Anne," I said through clenched teeth, "you are going to ruin something, and then we are both going to be sorry." My words did little to calm her. Finally, I grabbed her by the shoulders and "escorted" her to her room.

As we marched down the hall, I had a sudden flashback of myself as a young teen. I had almost forgotten that I'd kicked a door or two in those days.

Thinking quickly, I reached for the pillow on Tobi's bed. "You know, honey, I remember when I was angry, I used to feel like kicking things sometimes, so I understand your need to get your frustrations out. But if you feel like you just have to hit something, beat on something you can't hurt."

"Here," I told her, "you can punch your pillow to your heart's content." I handed her the pillow and left the room.

All was quiet for some time. I was just about to congratulate myself on my brilliant handling of the situation when I heard the muffled sound of fist meeting pillow again and again.

Nevertheless, Tobi emerged from her room a few minutes later, cool, calm, and collected. I smiled smugly to myself and forgot about the whole incident until about a week later. It was wash day and I was methodically stripping all the beds in the house. I came to Tobi's room and started taking the sheets off her bed. Stripping off the pillowcase, I found myself face to face with a larger-than-life portrait rendered directly onto the pillow in colorful marking pens.

Now, Tobi inherited some of her father's remarkable artistic talents, and this portrait was quite skillfully done. In fact, the face on the pillow looked familiar.

And then it struck me: I was looking into a "mirror." It was my own face staring back at me from the pillow!

As I pictured my daughter methodically drawing my likeness on her pillow and then beating the stuffing out of "me" with her fists, I laughed so hard I could barely finish the laundry. I couldn't help but be impressed with her creativity—and the willpower it must have taken not to show me her handiwork the day it was completed.

I have no doubt that her portrait punching bag was well used for the remainder of her years at home. (Just for the record, the only punishment we ever doled out for defacing the pillow came a few months later when brand-new pillows were purchased for the family during a K-mart white sale. I bought only five pillows for our six-member family. She didn't even have to ask why she wasn't the recipient of a new one.)

We've told that story many times since, and Tobi laughs loudest of all. She went away to college last fall, and I'm pretty sure her punching-bag pillow went with her. But I'd be willing to bet, from the sweetness and love we hear in her voice through the four-hundred miles of telephone wire, that nowadays that pillow gets hugged more than it gets hammered.

Dear Lord, teach me how to keep my head when I am angry with my children. Help my mind to work faster than my mouth. Show me how to teach my children to control their anger by setting a good example myself. Amen.

Get the Kid

Patsy Clairmont

Stop your anger! Turn from your rage!
Do not envy others—it only leads to harm.

Psalm 37:8 NLT

"Mommy, Mommy, Mommy, Mommy, Mommy, Mommy." Marty's persistence matched his rhythmic tugging on my blouse's hem.

I felt like screaming. In fact, I did.

To a little guy my response was probably similar to the release of Mt. St. Helens as I erupted, "What?!"

Why a mother waits so long to respond and allows the repetition to light her lava is beyond me. I only know that after spewing all over him, I felt terrible . . . and so did he.

Where did all this volcanic anger come from? I seemed to always be upset at something or someone.

Often my reactions were greater than the situation called for. I realized that Marty's little-child ways didn't deserve such strong responses.

Have you ever tried making things right when you know you're wrong but don't know how to admit it or quit it? That was often my frustration with Marty.

I'd send him to his room, leaving me with the realization that his punishment was greater than his crime. Then I'd try to make up by slipping him a Twinkie or playing a game with him. I soon found that Twinkies don't build good bridges of communication—to squishy.

During a prayer time, as I cried out to the Lord for help with my temper, especially with my son, an idea formed I believe was heaven-sent because it made a difference.

I was to pray with Marty before I administered any form of discipline. Sometimes those prayers sounded strange and strained as I almost shouted, "Dear Lord, help this miserable little boy and help this miserable mommy who wants so desperately to raise him in a way that would honor You."

By the time I said "amen," I was almost a reasonable person. I was able to see past my emotions and do what was in Marty's best interest.

Sometimes he needed a firm hand, but he was dealt with in love instead of anger, and the moment drew us together instead of tearing us apart. Many times all he needed was time and a mother's tender touch.

but one day that boy really ticked me off! I remember heading across the room for him like a high-speed locomotive, steam coming out all sides. I had one goal and intent—get the kid, get the kid, get the kid!

Just as I loomed over him, his eyes the size of saucers, he held up one hand and yelled, "Let's pray!"

Marty had learned a valuable lesson in life: "When Mommy talks to Jesus, we're all a lot better off."

Dear Lord, Sometimes when I am steamed, it seems that my kids know just which buttons to press. Help me to turn down the temperature with patience and prayer. Give me wisdom on how to discipline effectively without losing my cool. Help me to remember, in the heat of the moment, to stop and talk to You. Amen.

A Bed for Jasper

D. J. Note

Do not be anxious about anything, but in everything, by prayer and petition, with thanksgiving, present your requests to God.

Philippians 4:6

Jasper needed a bed to call his own. "A regular old cardboard box just isn't good enough," my daughter told me.

She suggested we invest in a soft, over-stuffed circular model with a convenient cutout entrance for her apricot-colored tabby.

"A store-bought pet bed is pretty pricey, Monica." I explained. "And it's possible Jasper might refuse to sleep in it."

"But Mom-m-m, Jasper deserves a bed of his own," she insisted. "He's special. P-l-e-a-s-e, Mom."

The plea in her big, slate-blue eyes reminded me of the special place Jasper held in her heart.

Since his arrival on Christmas Eve, Monica found Jasper a willing participant in afternoon tea parties of dry cat food and water. He appeared to enjoy the mid-morning rides in her bright-pink baby doll stroller. And tolerating her doll's blue and white plaid bonnet and cotton flannel nightie was worth all the homespun attention Monica lavished him with.

"Let's drive to the store and see what we can find," I suggested. "They have lots of boxes. Maybe it would be wise to try a cardboard box first."

On the way to the market, I suggested we pray.

"Lord, You know just the right bed for Jasper," Monica whispered. "Please help us find it."

The middle-aged clerk wore a large, full-length, white apron and a friendly smile. Returning his hearty grin, I explained what we were looking for. "I'll just take a look in the back," he said to Monica, tilting his glasses to focus through his bifocals. Then he hurried away to the storeroom in search of a box.

Monica's waning smile revealed her doubt about the store clerk's mission. But when he returned, we both stood in disbelief at the lovely wooden box he held in his hands. The helpful gentleman couldn't possibly have known the label pasted at one end of the box was God's perfect answer to our prayer.

Amidst luscious grapes, yellow melons, and sparkling sapphire-colored berries the word "JASPER" extended across the entire sticker, in bold red letters! Underneath, tiny print advertised "California's Finest Fruits."

"Ask, and ye shall receive . . ." I laughed.

"Oh-my-gosh!" Monica squealed. Wrapping her arms around my waist she said, "Thank You, Jesus! Thank You."

The clerk raised his thinning eyebrows over our giddy reaction to a plain wooden box.

"The box is for her kitty." Pausing briefly, I added, "His name is Jasper! How much do I owe you?" I asked, digging through my purse for my wallet.

"Nothing at all," he smiled. "It's yours."

We offered another round of gratitude to the sweet gentleman.

I threw my arm around Monica's shoulder, and with our box in tow, we giggled our way out of the store. Jasper had his perfect bed!

An unexpected miracle? Maybe. A coincidence? Never! A blessing? Absolutely!

Dear Lord, how privileged I am that I can come to You in prayer. I can bring any request to You, no matter how insignificant. How wonderful it is to have a Lord who cares for me so much that I may bring my deepest worries—or my smallest cares. Thank You for being there for me. Amen.

The Runaway

Bobbie Wilkinson

*Instruct a wise man and he will be
wiser still; teach a righteous man
and he will add to his learning.*

Proverbs 9:9

A Thanksgiving college application deadline, set
by the high school guidance counselor, approached
for my middle daughter in the fall of 1991. As any
parent who has been through this particularly high-
stress time in a child's life knows, tempers are often
short, and emotions are like a roller coaster for both
students and parents.

Being the most like me of my three daughters, Kelly
had engaged with me in a number of power struggles
during her years in the purgatory of adolescence—and
my coinciding years in the purgatory of being her

mother at that time. This particular fall was the most challenging for me.

As I did with Kelly's older sister, I made myself available to help in any way that I could, knowing how chaotic her life was with her academic load, her position as a class officer, yearbook editor, etc.

One particular afternoon, Kelly was at the computer working on one of her application essays. I was aware of the familiar danger signals warning me that she was not in a friendly mood. If looks could kill, I would have met my demise when she was in, oh, about the seventh grade.

I still don't remember exactly how our verbal exchange began. But I was in a good mood and recall simply asking if there was anything I could do for her. Things slid downhill rapidly until Kelly, the beloved child of my womb, used words that were so verbally abusive to me that I was almost paralyzed with shock.

I immediately realized I had a choice to make. I could reduce myself to her level and quite easily scream some expletives that were on the tip of my tongue. Or, I could remove myself from the scene of the crime. I chose the latter. Without saying a word, I

left the den and went up to my bedroom. I knew
what I was going to do. I got out my suitcase and
made the spontaneous decision to go away for a few
days. Mom was running away from home.

As I was finishing my packing, I heard my
husband's car come in the driveway. Kelly went
outside to greet him, crying hysterically. I could hear
what was going on, because my bedroom is right
above the driveway. I heard Kelly through her sobs
tell her father that she had said some terrible things to
me and that I would probably never forgive her. Tom
was his usual wonderful self in his role of father,
hugging and comforting her, yet trying also to find
out what exactly happened.

As I heard Kelly's sobs, I knew I could stop my
packing, go downstairs, hug Kelly, accept her apology,
and tell her everything was fine. But everything wasn't
fine, and I knew in my heart that it was important to
allow Kelly to really feel her pain if anything was to
be learned from this experience.

I continued my packing, then headed downstairs,
suitcase in hand, to announce that I was going away
for a few days. I wasn't angry, teary, or emotional. I

simply expressed my need to get away. My birthday happened to fall on one of the days I would be away, which was major, considering how we celebrate those events in our family.

I asked that no one buy any presents for me that year. The only gift I wanted was time away by myself.

I told no one but a close female friend where I was going, as I didn't want any connection with my family for the island of time I was away.

They would, of course, be able to reach me in an emergency; but I really wanted that time and space to be totally mine.

It was very quiet as I hugged everyone good-bye in our kitchen. I didn't admonish Kelly and tell her I wanted her to think about what she had said to me. She already knew. I just left in love, as if I had planned this trip for a while, instead of having just made the decision to leave within the hour.

Off I went to what remains an undisclosed location. I read by a warm fire every night. I crocheted an afghan that was to be a Christmas gift. I prayed. I took long walks. I journaled. I refilled the pitcher that was empty, the pitcher that was me.

Five days later, I quietly returned home, refreshed and refueled. Kelly was the only one home at the time. She gave me a hug and asked if she could talk to me in the living room. We went in and sat down, and she began to pull out a couple of presents for me. I reminded her of my request, but she said, "Mom, please open them."

The first was my favorite kind of scented candle, on which she had spent a good bit of her allowance and had driven thirty miles to buy in a specialty store. She didn't tell me that; but we live in the rural, northern Virginia countryside, and I knew where she had to go to get this candle. I was profoundly touched.

But I was totally unprepared for the next gift she handed me. It was a painting she had done while I had been gone. She had titled it *Now,* and gave me a little note with the following explanation:

Then, when I was little, I would smile and you were there, yes, to smile with me. When I cried, yes, you were there. You were there. It was simple and beautiful. Yes, uncomplicated and pure. I painted you pictures of flowers and sunlight, yes, and happiness. Then it changed, and I hurt you. I hurt you like I've never hurt anyone before. And that hurt me like I've never hurt before. To hurt the person who gave me life, who gave herself to me. I cried, and it was dark.

Now, I smile and yes, again you smile with me. I talk to you and love you. Yes, I love you. I gave you light for your birthday to replace the darkness. Yes, again I paint happiness for you.

I sat there with tears streaming down my cheeks as I looked at her abstract painting with its rich blues, greens, and bright yellows that remind me of a candle's flame. Her faint signature in pencil on the bottom said, "Love always, Kelly."

This, I have come to realize, was a deeply transforming moment. It reaffirmed the bond of love and respect between Kelly and me, a bond that today remains intact and intimate, heartwarming and fun.

I don't know for certain where that puff of instinct came from that led this mother to run away one terrible night; but I do know the outcome of my spontaneous leave of absence. Kelly and I were able to find and appreciate each other again in a deeper, more profound and honest way. And for that cherished gift, I am grateful every single day of my life.

Dear Lord, I need to value my children, but I also need to value myself. Help me to see that You love me, for You call me Your child. Though I never want to harm my family by leaving them, show me how to give them tough love, so they will also value me. Amen.

Just Like Mom

Vickey Banks

Join with others in following my example,
brothers, and take note of those who live
according to the pattern we gave you.

Philippians 3:17

"You must be Shirley's daughter! I knew it as soon
as I saw you. You look just like her!" How many times
have I heard that comment? I look into the mirror
and see a green-eyed blond looking back at me. I look
at my mother and see a blue-eyed brunette. Where is
the similarity? I've finally quit shaking my head in
puzzlement. I've heard the comments so often now
that I expect them. According to popular opinion, I
look, act, walk, talk, and smile just like my mother!
Fortunately, I like my mother. As a matter of fact, if

you tell me I remind you of my mother, I will smile and say, "Thank you." I consider it a compliment.

As a little girl, I would gaze at her in amazement when she put on her makeup. I watched her dip the little brush in water and then into the blue Mary Kay eye shadow. When she brushed it onto her eyes, it seemed like magic. I thought she was the most beautiful woman in the world.

Whenever I was sick, I could count on my mom to make it better. She always had strawberry Jell-O and Campbell's soup on hand for such occasions. I loved it when the soup was chicken and stars. Somehow seeing the little cream-colored stars floating about made the prospect of soup more exciting. Mom knew that.

I am no longer a little girl. I am staring forty in the face, but guess who I still want when I am sick? You guessed it—my mom. She has led a life worth imitating.

Ten years ago, I experienced a life-altering day. With my own mother close at hand, an amazing thing happened—I became a mother. You know what else? I had never needed my own mother more. Her presence was nothing short of a godsend those first few weeks at home. She brought me food, did my laundry, cleaned my house (nobody can clean house like my mom), and let me take naps while she covered my new daughter with lipstick kisses.

By the time my daughter, Casey, was four years old, people were already telling her, "You look just like your mommy." I would smile with pride. How sweet, I would think. However, one day she did something that grabbed my attention. I was walking behind her, when suddenly her chubby hands reached up and pulled her hair into a ponytail. She then began twisting it until finally stopping to hold it in one hand. I stopped walking. My mouth dropped open. My eyes widened. How many times had I done that exact thing?

In that instant, I was overcome by the obvious fact that Casey was (without even knowing it) copying my behavior. She looked just like me. It made me acutely aware that her little eyes were always upon me. Frankly, I found the realization frightening. What if my example was not always a good one?

From that day forward, the phrase "just like mom" became more than sweet. It became a motivating factor for my behavior. When my daughter hears

those words, I want her to think of them as a compliment. Oh, how I want to live a life worth imitating!

*Dear Lord, just as I imitate my parents,
so my children imitate me. May the impression
I make on the lives of my children be good and
healthy. May it also reflect the impression
You have made upon me. Amen.*

Wisdom

The character and history of each child may be a new and poetic experience to the parent, if he will let it.

Margaret Fuller

Mom with a Mission

Julie Sutton

I, even I, have spoken; yes, I have called him. I will bring him, and he will succeed in his mission.

Isaiah 48:15

"Spider-Man! Hurry! I need your help. There are radioactive blobs stuck to the kitchen floor, and if they aren't removed right away, our entire family could be destroyed!" If there's one thing my five-year-old superhero responds to with enthusiasm, it's being given a "mission."

He chooses his weapons from our under-the-sink arsenal: a green sponge and a pink plastic scrubber. Last time, it was a pair of makeshift scrub brush "skates" fastened onto his bare feet with shoelaces. Soon he is busy unarming bombs, saving the household from certain death. Petrified cereal is soaked and pried from its linoleum minefield; dangerous sticky Kool-Aid spots are deactivated; sugary deposits under the table are safely neutralized with our top-secret formula (a mixture of warm water and dishwashing liquid).

Even Spidey's baby brother has joined in the campaign against evil, as he takes up his own weapon (a wet rag) against the highly volatile, stubborn wall splatters that surround his high chair.

In the next room, Mom blithely wields her feather duster, smug and satisfied, secretly patting herself on the back for her ingenious manipulation of these sometimes-unruly little ones. How clever I am, she thinks to herself. I've made it all into a game. They're having the time of their lives—and I'm getting my floors scrubbed!

Meanwhile, up in Heaven, an angel turns to God with an amused countenance. "How did you manage to get her to do your will so easily? Look at her: changing diapers, picking up dirty socks . . . the same chores that so many consider drudgery. Yet there she is, grinning and humming to herself as if she couldn't be happier! What did you do?"

"It was nothing," the Lord winks fondly. "After all, it's not hard to motivate someone who has a mission in life."

Dear Lord, You are my hero! I put my trust in You. Help me to be a hero to my children as I complete Your mission to raise them. And may I teach them that You are the ultimate hero as You show them Your mission for their own life adventures! Amen.

Gordon's Gift

Anne Marie Goodrich

Everything God created is good,
and nothing is to be rejected if
it is received with thanksgiving.

1 Timothy 4:4

I was glad that my children didn't seem to notice the surroundings that seemed so dismal to me.

Gordon and Kelly were blissfully unaware of our lack of luxuries that cold December in 1983. They were busy with kindergarten and first-grade affairs and full of pre-Christmas energy and excitement. The little black-and-white television with its coat-hanger antenna blared endless commercials for toys and trinkets for the upcoming holiday.

It seemed each advertisement was punctuated by cries of, "Oh Mama, I want that for Christmas! Mom, do you think Santa will bring me one of those?"

My answers were always weak and non-committal—and I even told them that Santa fills their stockings, that the wrapped presents come from Mom. I didn't want them to be disappointed in old Saint Nick.

Still, nothing I said dampened their enthusiasm and anticipation.

I was the one who looked sadly around our old apartment and saw paint chipping from walls, threadbare carpet, the orange-crate coffee table. I tried not to show my increasing anxiety about my lack of Christmas money and busied myself with preparations anyway. Because our ornament collection was scanty at best, the children and I made construction paper chains as garland for our little tree, and I carefully cut out a cardboard star and covered it in foil for its crowning touch.

Gordon and Kelly thought our little Christmas tree was beautiful.

As grateful as I was for their obliviousness to our situation, I still worried. They might not notice how strapped we were, but what were they going to think on Christmas morning when they awoke to just a few small packages under the tree?

Christmas Day begins early with a five- and six-year old.

"Mom! Mom! Santa Claus came! Will you get up now?"

There was no more hiding—no sudden windfall had come my way. I pasted a smile on my face, got my cup of coffee, and settled onto the couch with a rock of anxiety firmly lodged in my stomach. Two little faces looked up at me, eager with excitement.

"Which one should we open first?"

I carefully pointed out two small gifts. I knew all the presents under that tree were practical items except for one toy I managed to buy for each child.

"Why don't you open those," I said and watched as paper was quickly torn off, only to reveal a package of underwear inside.

"Thank you, Mom," I heard their chorus. I could only manage a weak smile.

I felt close to tears by the time I pointed to Gordon's third gift, knowing it was just a package of undershirts. "I'm afraid that's not a very exciting present," I whispered apologetically as my six-year-old started pulling off ribbon.

Gordon finished tearing off the paper, held the cellophane package of T-shirts up high, and with heartfelt emotion he replied, "Oh, but Mom, I really needed these. Thank you, Mom!"

Suddenly our shabby and threadbare living room seemed filled with light. It wasn't the glow from our little aluminum star on the tree or even the tears that came to my eyes but my heart expanding with gratitude and love.

Somehow, in the midst of all my worries, I hadn't realized that my children were becoming such good people, not in spite of a lack of material things but maybe because of it.

My little boy couldn't have been too excited by one more package of undergarments, but somehow at his young age, Gordon had learned a kindness rare for his years.

Through the years I've forgotten many holidays, but I'll never forget that Christmas morning in 1983. My young son gave me a gift of graciousness—and a priceless memory that I'll treasure always.

Dear Lord, help me to receive my role
in life with thanksgiving. Sometimes life seems
as ordinary as a pair of socks. Help me to remember
my higher calling, to be an example, teacher,
and encourager to my children. Thank You
for the gift of their lives. Amen.

Velveteen Mom

You are the body of Christ, and
each one of you is a part of it.
1 Corinthians 12:27

As I lay in the hospital bed, a deluge of silent tears flooded away all my hopes of becoming a mother. I would never carry a child in my womb. I would never know the thrill of childbirth. I would never hold my own baby in my arms. Reality sank in—the hysterectomy had robbed me of these wonderful privileges. It was final: motherhood had eluded me.

I gingerly leaned over toward the bedside table for a tissue and my worn Bible. The Psalms had comforted me during other painful times of wondering if I'd ever be a mother; surely they could again. I had needed their calming effect after reading the vastly differing opinions regarding the possible negative effects of pregnancy when I was diagnosed with Multiple Sclerosis. Was it even wise to have a child? Later I soaked up the Psalms' strength when the divorce filed by my husband of fifteen years swallowed up my dreams of having children with the man I loved. Now this.

Wiping my tear-stained face, I read several Psalms before my eyes fastened upon Psalm 68:6, "God sets the lonely in families." A tiny gasp escaped my lips. I was single, living alone, and would never have children.

"God, are You promising me a place within an established family? Or in the family of God? I know I am already part of Your family." I wrote in my Bible margin, "Given to me by God 8/14/86 while in the hospital for a hysterectomy."

Lying there, gazing out the window at the front range of the Rockies, my thoughts traveled to the fun I'd been having with Ray Franz and his two young daughters he had raised alone for six years. Could God actually be giving me a promise regarding their family of three? Melissa had even innocently asked, "Will you be my new mommy?" turning Ray's ruddy complexion beet red. But even with that thrilling thought, I sadly told myself, *Stepmothering isn't real mothering.*

Fourteen months later, Ray and I were married. I cuddled on the plaid couch between Lindsey and Melissa after a day full of motherly duties, while Lindsey read one of their favorite books, *The Velveteen Rabbit.* The story of a stuffed bunny hopped playfully off the pages and filled me with delight. The little rabbit asked, "What makes a bunny real?"

The Skin Horse replied, "When a child loves a toy— not just during play, but all the time—it becomes real."

I thought about the hugs and kisses and "I love yous" that had smothered me since I married Ray. The tender moments as I tucked the girls into bed and sang songs to them. Fixing breakfasts, sack lunches, and dinners while teaching my stepdaughters to cook and bake. Holding each of them in my arms as she cried over some situation at school. Hearing them tell me, "We're glad we don't have to share you with any other children. We've got you all to ourselves!" I was certainly loved.

Then I remembered refereeing the girls' arguments, sometimes losing my own temper in the process, only to apologize regretfully. They could be angry at my authority when they didn't want to be held accountable. My cooking wasn't what they were used to—and I heard about it. Some of the shininess of being their "new mommy" had already worn off. Yet I knew I was loved.

I was real!

Tears shown in my eyes as I whispered, "I'm a Velveteen Mom, you know."

The girls' eyes lit up with profound recognition and they smiled. "You are!" they cried with laughter while embracing me happily.

And no one can take your realness away, Jo, no one.

Dear Lord, You have made me real! I am a real person, a real mom! Sometimes it feels like I'm climbing a mountain so tall that I'll never reach the top. Sometimes I lose my perspective. But You have taken me by my hand; You are leading me to the top. I know I will never see the view if I never climb the mountain. Thank You for this journey to the top! Amen.

Letting Go

A mother's job is to hold on tight before she lets go.

Anonymous

Family Dinner

Sara L. Smith

The righteous eat to their hearts' content.

Proverbs 13:25

My sons are already home from high school when I arrive from the grocery store.

Aaron hangs up the telephone and pulls a box of cereal from one of the bags.

"There are more groceries in the car," I announce.

Both boys head out the door, shoving and bickering. At seventeen and fifteen, they're nearly full grown. I take a large beef roast from one of the bags. Pot roast is a special treat.

In past years, I routinely prepared a nice meal for dinner, the only time of the day when our family of seven could be together. Gradually, though, that time has been eroding. One or more of us is absent from the table nearly every night. My part-time job as a school cafeteria worker has depleted my enthusiasm for cooking at home. We've been eating a lot of soup and sandwiches lately.

But tonight is going to be like old times. I'm almost positive everyone will be home. I set seven large potatoes on the counter.

The boys jostle their way back into the kitchen with the rest of the groceries. Aaron shoves three gallons of milk into the refrigerator, breaks two bananas from the bunch, and pours himself a bowl of cereal.

John picks up a package of macaroni and cheese and begins heating a pan of water. "What's for dinner?" he asks me suspiciously while I slice onions over the meat.

"Pot roast, baked potatoes, carrots, salad, and marble cake."

"Do you have to put disgusting onions on the meat?"

"That's the way Dad likes it."

"What kind of icing for the cake?"

"I thought I'd make peanut butter," I say. I get a look of distaste in response.

Laura arrives home from middle school. Simultaneously, the telephone rings. "Is Laura there?" inquires a voice of indeterminate gender.

I give her the phone.

"Bye, Mom," Aaron says.

"Wait a minute," I call. "Where are you going?"

"Work. I'll be home at nine."

"But I thought you were off today."

"This is my Friday to work."

I put one of the potatoes back.

Laura hangs up after an unusually short conversation. "What's for dinner?"

I tell her. "Do you want to make the cake?"

She shakes her head. "Why can't we have pizza?"

"You had pizza for school lunch," I remind her. "I scraped cheese off hundreds of trays."

The telephone rings. It's a girl for Aaron. Laura takes the message.

Ten-year-old Karen and Dana, twenty, arrive together. Karen has a proud grin. "Dana gave me a ride home from school."

"I picked her up about a block away," Dana explains.

The telephone rings. "It's Christina." Dana hands the receiver to Laura.

"You're home from work early, aren't you?" I ask Dana.

"A little." She inhales the aroma of the roasting meat and onions that is permeating the kitchen. "Something smells good."

I recite the dinner menu once again.

"Eddie and I are going out to eat," Dana informs me.

I put another potato back.

"Yeah, he called me too," Laura is saying into the telephone. "He is so-o-o stupid."

Dana and I roll our eyes at each other and smile. She was thirteen herself not too long ago.

"Can I help you make the cake?" Karen asks.

"Sure."

We get out the mixing bowl and beaters. Karen greases the pan while I set the oven thermostat. "Marble cake is a little harder to make," I explain.

"I like chocolate better," Karen says wistfully.

"I like white better," Laura announces. Christina has her on hold.

"Well, I like marble," I tell them. "And so does your dad. With peanut butter icing."

Karen breaks the eggs. I pick out the pieces of shell. Karen measures the water. I measure the oil.

"Mom, may I go to Christina's house?" Laura asks.

"I guess so," I answer. "Be home at six." I turn on the mixer.

We pour the batter in the pan. "Want to lick the bowl?" I offer.

Karen hesitates, then shakes her head no.

I set the oven timer, then go to fold some laundry. Dana is in the shower. John is playing video games and eating macaroni and cheese out of the pan. The telephone rings. "He's at work," I hear Karen saying.

I take a knife and head out to the garden. There's enough fresh lettuce for salad. The telephone rings.

"Mom," John calls from the kitchen window. "May I go to the gym with Jerry?"

"What time would you get home?"

A pause while John asks for the information. "Eleven. Jerry wants to know if I can spend the night."

"All right," I agree, sighing.

Back in the house, I put another potato back. The cake is done, and I set it aside to cool while I mix up the icing.

"Couldn't we have mashed potatoes instead of baked?" Karen coaxes.

"Well . . ." I prefer mashed myself, and I'll have plenty of gravy. Now that our numbers are down to four, it wouldn't be that much more work. "No," I decide. "Dad likes baked.

I wash the lettuce carefully. One little bug and the kids won't touch garden lettuce all year. The telephone rings.

"Mom, it's my coach," Karen says.

"We're having a makeup game this evening," the softball coach tells me.

I groan.

"Sorry about the short notice, but I really need Karen tonight," he goes on. "Can you have her at the field by 5:30?"

"She'll be there," I say without enthusiasm.

I put another potato back.

"You'll have to get your uniform out of the laundry hamper," I tell Karen. "I'll fix you a toasted cheese sandwich."

The doorbell chimes while I'm making the sandwich. It's Ed, Dana's boyfriend. "What time will you be home?" I ask Dana.

"Late. We're seeing a movie."

I scrape carrots to put in with the meat. My husband, Ron, and I love carrots done this way, so I prepare the entire package. The telephone rings.

"Could you please tell Aaron that Jenny called?" asks a soft feminine voice.

I add the note to Aaron's other messages: Heather called, Melissa called, Amy called, Lisa called.

"I'm ready," Karen announces.

I look at her. "Wash your face. Get your hat. And where's your glove?"

The telephone rings. It's Laura.

"Mom, could I eat dinner with Christina?"

"But I made a cake," I protest. "Maybe Christina would like to eat over here."

"Please," Laura begs. "They're ordering a pizza."

"All right," I snap. "Be home at eight."

I put another potato back. Then I wrap the remaining two potatoes with foil and set them in the oven. I arrange the carrots around the meat. The roast is browning nicely and smells delicious.

I drive Karen across town to the ball field, sulking the whole way. *So much for my nice family dinner! Why did I bother?*

Ron is home from work when I get back to the house. "Where is everybody?" he asks.

"Dana had a date, Aaron is working, John went to the club with Jerry, Laura is eating with Christina, and Karen had a makeup game."

"So it's just the two of us for dinner?" Ron gives me a wicked grin. I manage a smile. "I told Karen we'd come to the ball field later."

"What smells so good?"

"Pot roast and carrots."

"Mmmm." His face lights up eagerly. "You put onions on too?"

"Sure."

"And baked potatoes?"

"Yep. And salad and marble cake." By now my grin feels genuine too.

"With that good icing I like?"

"Naturally." I start into the kitchen, but Ron stops me, catching me in a big hug and kiss.

"So you made this nice meal just for me?"

I hug him back. "Of course."

Dear Lord, may I not neglect my spouse as I try to be a good mother. For what I want to save for my old age is my marriage. Help me not to allow the distractions of life to break up a beautiful romance. Teach me how to make time for my partner. Amen.

The Big Yella Fella

Dr. Linda Karges-Bone

I made you grow like a plant of the field.
You grew up and developed and
became the most beautiful of jewels.

Ezekiel 16:7

During the weeks preceding my daughter Carolyn's first day of school, I did everything right. That's just the way I do things. Her hair was trimmed into a perfect auburn bob. Her backpack was sturdy yet fashionable. We attended "meet the teacher" and (with a few tears) got the right immunizations.

Carolyn, with her usual stoic nature, expressed a bit of worry about this major change in her life, but I was unfailingly enthusiastic. I mean, why not? I had spent six years teaching in both public and private schools and then moved on to earn a doctorate in education.

Good grief! I made my living by preparing teachers at the college level and writing books and articles for parents and teachers. This school thing was a piece of cake, and I knew every crumb of it.

The first day of school was going to be a perfectly coordinated, flawless transition for my brilliant little girl. I hadn't counted on the fact that I would be the problem. It was all the fault of "The Big Yella Fella."

No, we weren't attacked by a fierce dog on the way to school. It was the school bus that did me in.

No, I wasn't run over in some sort of freak accident. It was the very sight of the "Big Yella Fella," as the kids call their school bus, that reduced me to a blubbering, blithering mess of motherhood.

Having made the decision to let Carolyn begin first grade by riding our neighborhood school bus, we waited patiently at the end of our comfortable middle-class cul-de-sac on a sunny August morning. I had already taken an entire series of pictures to record the event. Carolyn on the front porch—without her backpack. Carolyn on the front porch—with her backpack and lunch box. Carolyn and her baby sister on the front porch. Carolyn waiting at the bus stop.

We were out of film by that point, which was just as well, because the bus could be heard rumbling around the corner.

Carolyn was excited, hopping from one foot to the other, her eyes shining. I was smiling, the epitome of a calm, assured adult—until I saw the beast. It was not a school bus at all. It was an enormous, yellow monster with a gaping hole of a door that was about to swallow up and steal away my precious firstborn.

It has been ten years since that day, and I can still bring back that feeling of horror and paralyzing fear. I wanted to pick that child up in my arms and run right back home to our safe, protected world where I was in charge (or so I thought) of everything. Home, where Carolyn's schedule, her friends, her choices were really mine to make and defend. I didn't want her to get on the yellow beast and go away to that dangerous place they call school.

All sorts of terrible thoughts rushed through my mind. What if terrorists overran the playground? What if she was exposed to a dangerous virus? What if she was exposed to bizarre spiritual teaching? Worst of all, what if someone hurt her feelings?

The bus stopped. I felt Carolyn pulling her hand away from mine. I heard her saying, "Look Mommy. The Big Yella Fella is here. It's time to go, Mommy."

Quickly, I blinked back tears. I gulped down a wave of terror so that my voice sounded something like normal. "Wow!" I replied with false gaiety. "The Big Yella Fella for my big girl. Let's go big girl!"

In a move that seemed to shock the bus driver, I not only walked her up the bus steps but quickly walked through the bus checking for terrorists, dangerous broken springs in seats, or unsavory-looking characters who might have hidden on the bus in the night. All things seemed normal, so I was forced to get off the bus.

Carolyn was waving, her freckled nose pressed against the window. The Big Yella Fella rumbled off. When the bus rounded the bend onto Simmons Avenue, I lost it.

I remember collapsing into a heap amid a bed of impatiens at the end of our lane and sobbing uncontrollably. I couldn't stand to let go of my baby. My sobs were so loud and despairing that they drew out the attention of my neighbor Kathy. Her children were a little older, and she was a little wiser. Assessing the situation in a glance, she patted my shoulder and wryly said, "I knew you weren't so tough. It'll get better," she laughed and then added, "they'll have to medicate you when the kid goes to college."

It has gotten better. When her baby sister, Audrey, went to school, I drove her for the first few days, knowing the risk that the Big Yella Fella holds for a cowardly mom like me. Most of all, I have learned to begin every school day with prayer. That way, even though I am not on the bus, I know I am not sending my children out into the world alone. I am learning to let go.

Dear Lord, as I send my children out into the world, teach me how to let go. I know that there is no teacher greater than life experience. I do my best to pass my experience down to my children, but I know they must learn from their own experiences as well. Keep them safe in this process! Amen.

Remember Me

B e t t y   J .   J o h n s o n

I will receive you. I will be a Father to you,
and you will be my sons and daughters.

2 Corinthians 6:17-18

"Mom will recognize me today," I said to my husband as we parked in front of the nursing care center. "Somehow, I just know she will."

For the previous six months I had lived with a gut-wrenching feeling of rejection. My own mother didn't know me. The horrible disease called Alzheimer's had robbed Mom of her memory and stolen the mother I once knew. Now, I was desperately trying to convince myself that this visit would be different.

The previous week, when our children admired the six-foot Christmas tree decorating our Colorado home, it triggered a memory in me of Mom's little

"Charlie Brown" trees—the bargains she bought for us on Christmas Eve afternoons. Remembering, I turned to my husband and whispered, "Could we drive to Iowa next week? I really need to see Mother."

Now I was at the care center, and it was time to face reality. With mixed feelings, I pushed open the heavy door and turned toward Mom's room. There she sat, wearing her favorite pink and white polka-dot blouse, the one we had bought together several years before.

I walked directly to this little woman, so frail but still mobile. Reaching down and taking her arm, I gently lifted her from the chair and said, "Hi Mom. We came to take you for a ride."

Please, Lord, let her show some sign of recognition—just a smile or that special light in her eyes, I silently prayed.

Mom looked up, smiled, and said, "OK!"

"OK"—a simple two-letter word, but it sounded like a two-hundred voice chorus singing to me. And there was that beloved smile.

We slowly walked to the car and rode around the lake. "Look, Mom, the sun still sparkles on the water just like it always has," I commented. "And the green pastures of our farm still look inviting."

Focusing on God's unchanging creation reminded me of His unchanging love.

The feelings of rejection diminished, and there was a new sense of peace in my heart as we finished our afternoon drive. I knew that the special smile of recognition and the simple word "OK" were beautiful gifts for one special day. I also knew that my mother's love was still tucked within her heart, even when she couldn't remember my name.

𝒟ear Lord, even though my own mother may not be able to remember me, You never will forget me. Thank You that, even when our memories fade, Your love never fails. You are my rock and anchor. I will put my trust in You. Help me to feel Your love for me. Amen.

School Days

Nancy B. Gibbs

Your decrees are the theme of
my song wherever I lodge.

Psalm 119:54

My children's first day of kindergarten came much too quickly for me. The entire time that my twin sons were getting ready and while they ate breakfast, I sang the song "School Days." I don't know if I sang it for the boys to laugh at, or if I was simply singing if for myself. The louder I sang, the less likely I was to cry. I guess it was a coping method for me.

The first day of the first grade was quickly upon us. Again, the morning was filled with my off-key version of "School Days."

"Oh, Mama," the boys would say, while fighting back the smiles.

SCHOOL DAYS

Every year on the first day of school, the scene was the same. Second grade, third, fourth, fifth, all the way up to the twelfth grade. I didn't care whether they liked it or not. The more they opposed, the louder I sang (and the worse it sounded).

Tears filled my eyes as I sang to them on the first day of the twelfth grade.

I knew that the next year they would be off at college, and I probably wouldn't see them on the first day. Even though I was ready for them to grow up, there were many things for which I wasn't ready—like the empty nest.

The night before the first day of their college classes, Chad called home from his apartment. He was excited and wanted to share with me all about his new books and the professors he had met. Before we hung up, Chad said, "Classes start at 8:00 tomorrow, Mama. Are you going to call me? We have to leave at 7:30."

"Do you want me to call, Son?" I asked.

"Yes, Mama, I do," Chad said. "You have to sing 'School Days.'"

"What if I just go ahead and sing it tonight?" I asked.

"But it just won't be the same," Chad declared.

At 7:00 sharp the next morning, I called singing "School Days" to both of the boys on the phone. They were laughing as we hung up.

After I placed the receiver back on the hook, tears filled my eyes. I realized that children cherish some traditions, and that, oftentimes, they live on. I have a feeling that "School Days" will ring loud and clear in my sons' homes when my future grandchildren start to school.

Dear Lord, thank You for the children You have blessed me with—that they would cherish a family tradition, even as young adults. As they grow into adulthood, please instill in them the traditions of wisdom and love that come from knowing and following You. Amen.

Grandmothers

Dearer than our children,
are our children's children.

Egyptian Proverb

Grandma Got Lost!

Nancy G. Carter

"'We had to celebrate and be glad, . . .
he was lost and is found.'"

Luke 15:32

Rachel was my first grandchild, and I was there at the hospital when she was born. It took only one look at that adorable little face to change me from a normal woman to a woman who would accost strangers with baby pictures. I would have set up my projector and screen at the local mall if the security guard wouldn't have stopped me!

Rachel and I grew to have a wonderful relationship. She loved to cuddle in my lap while I read to her. One weekend I read her all of her favorite stories,

"The Three Little Pigs," "The Three Bears," and "Little Red Riding Hood." Soon I ran out of stories to read. I asked, "Would you like to hear a story about me when I was a little girl?"

"Oh, yes Grandma," she said, her eyes shining.

I told her, "One hot summer day, when I was about your age, I was playing on the front porch. Soon I wandered off the porch and started walking, hoping to find the ice-cream store. I went so far I didn't know how to get back home. I was so afraid.

"When my mother and father discovered I was missing, they were frantic. My father thought I had been kidnapped. My mother organized a crew of older neighborhood children to search for me. Finally, a boy found me about a mile away."

I ended the story with a moral. "Be careful, Rachel. Never go for a walk all by yourself."

All through that weekend, Rachel asked me to repeat the story to her. Each time I told it, she listened, her little face very serious as I went over the details.

When my daughter came to pick her up that Sunday night, she couldn't wait to tell her about

Grandma getting lost! Now Rachel turned on the drama. As she began telling the story, I realized she was actually experiencing the terror of my ordeal! When she came to the part of my realizing I was lost and frightened, her little voice broke and she began sobbing, "And, Mommy, Grandma was lost and couldn't find her mommy!"

My daughter Robin smiled and hugged Rachel and said, "But honey, Grandma did find her way home or she wouldn't be here today!"

I smiled and wiped away a tear from my eye, for I suddenly felt the love my little granddaughter had for me—a love that could cry for concern over her grandma who had been lost over forty years before!

What a love! What a granddaughter! Would you care to see her picture? Hold on for a minute while I haul my wallet out of my purse.

𝔇ear Lord, grandparenting is an amazing job at a wonderful time of life. Though it shows my age, I love it. Thank You for every grandchild blessing You send my way. Amen.

The Keepsake

Jan Coleman

A good man leaves an inheritance
for his children's children.

Proverbs 13:22

"Now, take your time, honey," my father said, turning the key below the tarnished brass doorknob. "Your grandmother wanted you to have the first choice; after all, you were her favorite."

It was 1968, and we had just buried Grandma a few days before. This was the first time in my twenty years that I would enter the tidy little house and not find her smile greeting me at the door. I lingered on the porch for a moment, avoiding as long as I could the task that would disturb the setting of happy childhood memories.

"Choose a keepsake you can hand down to your own children someday," Dad said. "Like the Seth Thomas clock or maybe the old 1930s radio. Some of her jewelry might be nice. You could have the stones reset, and you'd be wearing a reminder of her."

It was difficult to begin when I was still grieving for the woman who could soothe my adolescent anguish with a warm hug and a plate of gingersnaps. Because my mother's inner struggles drew her to alcohol and away from me, I drifted closer to Grandma, her contentment and easy way a soothing magnet for a troubled girl.

She was most at home in her kitchen, hovering over the huge Wedgewood stove, surveying the state of her plump pies as she wiped her doughy hands on a red checkered apron. The aroma of cinnamon and crisp Pippin apples percolated through the room as she'd dispatch me to the yard to climb the tree and pluck a few more. "We'll make tarts just for us," she'd say. "Let's not tell Grandpa."

Drifting from room to room, I was absorbed with thoughts of that house soon to be bare, all traces of my grandparents gone, their hodgepodge of furnishings dispersed to family members who would pass them down again and again until nobody remembered where they came from. I thought about how someday I would have children. I was sad that they would never know her, the greatest influence on my youth.

Pausing in the living room, my fingers stroked the old melodeon, a handsome pump organ where Grandma would sit after dinner every holiday, banging out endless melodies of Christmas carols and old hymns. We all stood behind her, balancing our mugs of eggnog while crooning along. What a prize that piece would be but merely a dust collector for a girl who inherited no musical gift. That would best be left to one of my cousins who did.

The massive oak table dwarfed the small dining room when it was extended with all the leaves necessary for our family celebrations. As I set the table, Gram reminded me that this handmade treasure was a wedding present from her parents. No doubt a grand treasure to last many lifetimes, but I had no place for it. The oldest cousin had just married and had the perfect spot in his house.

I thought perhaps one of the oil paintings on the wall would be a fitting keepsake. The artist was Grandpa's mother who came to California from Missouri in a Conestoga wagon in 1864 when just a child. The frames alone were priceless, but they would have to be in storage for such a long time while I finished college, and another cousin was studying art and had mentioned years before how he'd like to have them.

I stood in the bedroom, the afternoon sun filtering through dainty lace curtains that accented the weeks of dust on the highboy dresser. *Wasn't it only yesterday that she tucked me in the big poster bed when I stayed the weekend?* Kissing me good night, her fleshy cheek felt so soft against mine, such a contrast to her small, frail body that grew weaker when she was finally bedridden. What a striking bed it was, rich walnut wood standing tall off the floor, draped with a colorful quilt. I thought that piece would be something to hand down to a daughter one day, who would cherish those cozy nighttime prayers as I did.

Last, I took a peek in the den. A tattered red sofa bed, a painted metal file cabinet, a desk. Above it hung a framed cross-stitch from the Bible, "Do not store up for yourself treasures on earth where moth and rust destroy, but lay up for yourselves treasures in heaven." How many times had I darted in and out of that room and never pondered on the verse, the message to her family?

I flung open the closet door. Yes, it was still there, the best keepsake of all, and I almost missed it. I was barely thirteen the day she brought the cardboard box down from the shelf. "Let me show you what I do when Grandpa goes to bed." There were hundreds of typewritten articles, stories, and poems, all neatly labeled in manila envelopes.

"I was just a little tot during the San Francisco earthquake, but I wrote a story about it," she said. "And your grandpa and I struggled to raise a family through the Great Depression, so I wrote articles on practicing that attitude of gratitude. And I had some good suggestions on how to be a good neighbor."

I watched her relive our family history as she opened each marked envelope. "You know, during the second World War, women went to work in factories. Why, your Aunt Dessie repaired ships at the naval yard, and she was a real-life Rosie the Riveter. She's a character in this little yarn. And, sweetie, does your dad ever talk about his combat years? He was on the beaches of Normandy on D-Day, but of course I didn't know it until it was over. What a time to be a mother. There was never a shortage of things to write about."

I was much too young then to realize the value of what she was bequeathing me. A chronicle of her life, tales woven from her unique perspective, her passion, and her prayers.

"I want you to have these when I'm gone, so they won't end up stuffed in somebody's attic. You're a storyteller, and a talented one too."

When my father saw me carrying the tattered box out to the car, he looked puzzled. I couldn't explain it at the time, that I didn't want anything else, that I'd found the best prize of all.

That box sits on a shelf in my closet now, and I've guarded it for almost thirty years. The yellowing pages still brighten my spirits when I think of the author. Without my grandmother's gentle influence, I may never have viewed my difficulties as character builders and never understood that without forgiveness, I would never be free.

THE KEEPSAKE

It was many years later that I had my first story published, and when I saw my byline in that magazine, I whispered, "This one's for you, Gram."

I am writing those stories from my life for my grandchildren. I hope to teach them all the things she taught me and that a true inheritance is something moth and rust can never destroy. It's a legacy of love.

Dear Lord, may my life be a legacy to my children and to my children's children. May I spend it in a way that will reward those who come after me with a legacy of love. Thank You for this rich opportunity. Amen.

Laughter and Life Jackets

N. C. Haas

"Greater love has no one than this,
that he lay down his life for his friends."

John 15:13

"Who is this?" my friend asked, pointing to the snapshot of the little boy looking back from my refrigerator door.

"Oh, he's just a child we know," I answered, smiling.

When she had gone, I looked again at the picture and laughed. He was such a captivating little boy, with a bright impatient look that commanded, "Hurry with that camera! I have adventures to live and treasure to find, giants to capture and pirates to hunt!"

Who knew what great heroic plan his imagination had concocted the day that picture was taken! Whatever it was, he was completely prepared to accomplish it in the outrageous outfit he had rigged for himself: a baseball cap, oversized sunglasses, bedroom slippers, and, last but not least, a life jacket! How could I help but laugh? His energy bounded from that snapshot as though it were going to vault him right off the refrigerator and into my kitchen!

I could hardly believe he was already three years old, though I remembered his beginnings like they were yesterday. His father and mother, Scott and Lisa, were young and unmarried when he was conceived. While Lisa was still making college choices, Scott was already a sophomore thinking ahead to graduate school. Too frightened to share their "secret," they guarded it as long as they could, groping alone for a solution, any way out of their painful predicament.

They knew as soon as their secret was told, they would face the overwhelming reality of crushed dreams and agonizing decisions. They wanted a family but not that way. They believed children needed the solid foundation of a strong marriage but didn't know if they could build one together.

They could have ended the pregnancy. Others had. No one would have known. It would have been so simple to start again, as though nothing had changed. But, simple as it seemed, God would know. Whatever the consequences, they chose to give their baby life.

Finally, they braced themselves for what their news might bring. Disappointment and hurt from parents, shock and whispers from church friends—and more paralyzing questions. How would they afford medical care when Lisa had no insurance? How could she raise a child and return to school if she and Scott didn't marry? How would Scott manage the financial responsibilities of pregnancy and parenting?

They moved robotically through the next weeks. Scott left college, unsure if he would ever return. He found work as a waiter, while Lisa trudged from door to door, looking for anyone who would hire a young pregnant girl with little experience and no degree.

Their list of options grew more complicated. Should their parents raise the child? Should they consider adoption? Nothing seemed ideal. Meanwhile they continued through their own bittersweet moments of pregnancy—the sonogram that showed they had a son, the first sounds of his heartbeat, his first rustling movements.

But, as Lisa grew larger, their deadlines pressed on them with relentless urgency. Staggered by decisions only they could make, they pored over detailed files of hopeful adoptive couples, searching for one to whom they might entrust their child. How could they choose?

Their parents struggled, too, smiling bravely at pictures of other people's grandchildren; stifling tears at baby showers; worrying first that Scott and Lisa wouldn't marry, then worrying they would; uncertain how to parent—holding too tight, then forcing themselves to let go; wondering where they had failed; always asking God to be present with His love and His will.

Finally, one bright summer morning, Scott and Lisa's beautiful son was placed in their arms. Clinging to his soft warmth, they were torn again. But there was no time left; they had to decide. The next days were the most painful of all. While their parents asked God for His perfect will, Scott and Lisa struggled tearfully.

Then, bravely determining what they believed was best for their son, they dressed him, took him to a small church to dedicate him to God, then to the agency to give him to the couple they had chosen to parent him.

The terrible conflict of letting go and holding tight ripped through their hearts. They faced months of heartache, endless moments of wondering.

Time moved them all back to life's healing routine. All that remained was a chapter of memories, a closet full of ongoing prayers, and, occasionally, a picture and letter from the agency updating Scott and Lisa.

It was an extra picture they had given me that now hung on my refrigerator and made me laugh each time I saw it. It was much too small to contain this three-year-old package of comical energy bursting with so much busy excitement. He really did look as though, at any moment, he would leap right into my morning, scoop me into his adventure, and dare me to keep up.

Oh yes, I laughed back at his eager face, *how I would love it if you did! I would catch you up in my arms and twirl you around and around—life jacket, baseball cap,* sunglasses, and all! We would spin and laugh together, at the giants you had conquered and the pirates you had caught. We would spin, spin, and laugh again—at the fading memory of the pain that birthed you, at the wonder of the world before you. We would laugh until we cried in raucous celebration of your life.

And when we had spun ourselves dizzy, I would put you down, kneel in front of you and tell you this: Right now you can't see, but God has built bigger plans into your heart and promises into your soul than you can ever imagine. Your life is His, and your greatest adventure will be to discover Him and go with Him to find His purpose and plans for you. They are exciting plans, I promise, full of wonderful hope and purpose. Go and capture them. Go and live them. And don't forget your life jacket, Nathaniel—my first grandchild.

Dear Lord, despite my own disappointments, may I lay down my life for my family. May my love for them be greater than earthly treasures. Give me the courage to make sacrifices when needed and to lay down my own will for Yours. Amen.

243

Grandmother's Quilt

Linda Evans Shepherd

*As a mother comforts her child,
so will I comfort you.*

Isaiah 66:13

When we received word that my ninety-seven-year-old grandmother, Sue Leland, had passed away in her sleep, my nine-year-old son's eyes misted. "Why did she have to die?" he asked.

I pulled him onto the sofa to sit with me as we snuggled together, wrapped in my grandmother's Scripture quilt. The beautiful quilt originally had been made for Sue's mother, my great-grandmother, by her circle of friends from church. Each unbleached ivory square had been embroidered carefully with favorite Scriptures, then signed before being bordered with brightly colored triangles cut from flour sacks.

I put my arm around my son. "Grandmother's life was as rich and beautiful as this quilt," I explained, touching the blue, pink, and lavender calico. "She loved to teach from the Scriptures. See, here's her favorite verse."

My fingers slid down to the square my grandmother had stitched in neat blue letters when she was but a girl. Together we read Psalm 56:11 KJV: "In God have I put my trust: I will not be afraid what man can do unto me."

I looked down at my son, "She is with God now," I explained. "He was the center of her life. She always longed for the day she would meet Him face to face."

He smiled through his tears. "I'm glad for her," he said.

At that moment, the scraps of fabric, hand sewn four generations earlier, were more than a beautiful quilt. They were a handwritten letter from a boy's great-grandmother to her great-grandson and will continue to be a remarkable legacy of faith and love for generations to come.

Dear Lord, may I leave behind a legacy of faith. May my children pass on this heritage to their children. May their faith be assuring and enduring to make a difference in the lives of those around them. Amen.

What's a Grandma to Do?

Patricia Lorenz

*I do not want to see you now and make
only a passing visit; I hope to spend
some time with you, if the Lord permits.*

1 Corinthians 16:7

*O*ne of the most pressing problems for grandparents
these days is knowing how to be a grandparent. I
certainly don't wear cotton flowered dresses and full-
size aprons and bake molasses cookies every week like
my grandma Kobbeman did. I don't sit on a porch
swing and rock the evenings away or watch soap
operas like my grandmother Knapp did. After I
became a grandmother, I water-skied behind my
brother's boat in Kentucky and snorkeled for hours in

the ocean off the coast of two Hawaiian Islands. The next year I rode every scary roller coaster at Disneyland.

Grandmothers (and grandfathers) are different nowadays. We have full-time careers. We run corporations and marathons. We belong to clubs, watch the stock market, eat out a lot, exercise regularly, and still have time to do the Macarena.

My four grandchildren live out of town, and I don't see them on a regular basis. In fact, since their parents all have busy careers and whirly-gig lives like I do, I'm lucky if I get to see my grandchildren once every month or two.

When Hailey was four years old, she came for her very first "all alone" visit. She would be alone with me from Saturday night till Tuesday afternoon, when her mother would arrive to take her home. Saturday night and Sunday were a breeze. Hailey, her favorite blankie, the latest Beanie Baby, and I snuggled together in my big bed. We slept just fine until Hailey sat up in the middle of the night and whispered, "Gramma, you were snoring."

All day Sunday we kept busy with my daughter-in-law and other granddaughter who were visiting for the day. But on Monday morning when Miss Hailey and I woke up and she assured me that I didn't snore at all that night, I began to fret. I had books to read and review and a book proposal to get out. I needed to be in my office! How was I ever going to get it all done if I had to entertain Hailey all day?

I'll worry about it later, I thought. For at that moment, there were little girl hugs to be had, waffles to pop in the toaster, and birds to feed on the deck with my four-year-old helper.

And so we hugged and rocked and ate. I held the bird feeder while Miss Hailey scooped up six big cupfuls of tiny seed into the feeder, only a half-a-cup or so landing on the carpet.

As we sat in the glider swing on the deck, watching the squirrels eat the bird feed, I began to worry again. I had a column to write and a talk to prepare. Yet I wanted so much to be with Hailey. After all, we only had a day-and-a-half left before her mother would come. But my work, I needed to work. Or did I?

"Grammie, can we put up the hammock? Remember last summer when we watched the squirrels from the hammock? We could take a nap in it!"

"Let's go to the shed and find that hammock," I said gleefully. We hung the chains into the hooks in the big trees in the backyard and hopped aboard. We watched a yellow finch and two cardinals flit around the branches high above us as we lay on our backs in that big, double-wide hammock, and I knew for certain that I was taking the next day-and-a-half off work—completely.

Hailey and I drew huge pictures on the driveway, using up a whole bucketful of sidewalk chalk. Then she wanted to climb up into her Uncle Andrew's old tree house. She swept all the leaves off the tree-house floor, and half of them landed on my head. We took a long bike ride on the path near my house. I walked while Hailey rode her tiny two-wheeler with the training wheels.

"Grammie, can we go down by the creek?" Miss Hailey squealed when she saw the water.

"Sure! Maybe we'll catch a frog!"

Later that morning we jumped in the car, went shopping for shoes, and found just the perfect pair for my wide-footed grandchild. Then we headed to the playland at McDonald's for lunch. Later that afternoon, we ate popcorn and candy at the $1.99 movie as we giggled at the funny songs in *Cats Don't Dance.*

"Grammie, are you sure there aren't any rules at your house?"

"I'm sure."

"No bedtime?"

"Nope."

"I can stay up until you go to bed?"

"Yup."

"Until late?"

"Sure. We can sleep late tomorrow. You just sit here in my lap, so we can snuggle, and I'll read you a couple of books."

"I love you, Grammie."

And that's how I learned the true meaning of the words I have laminated on top of my computer: Write things worth reading or do things worth writing.

I learned that doing things like spending an entire day-and-a-half playing with a granddaughter is infinitely more important than sticking to a work routine and getting things done in the office. I learned that grandmothers today often need to abandon their schedules, meetings, clubs, activities, workload, and appointments and spend hours at a time drawing silly animals on the driveway or staring at the leaves from a hammock with a four-year-old's head snuggled in the crook of an arm.

Dear Lord, just about the time I thought my work was done, I became a grandmother. Thank You for this awesome privilege. Help me find the joy in watching my grandchildren grow into fine adults. Show me the best way to make a positive difference in their lives. Amen.

Silent Disapproval

Suzy Ryan

Bear with each other and forgive whatever grievances you may have against one another. Forgive as the Lord forgave you.

Colossians 3:13

In high school, I orchestrated my popularity as a politician campaigns for votes. Everyone admires cheerleaders, right? Since I wanted to be liked, I used that notoriety to ensure acceptance. Yet what I really craved was the approval of my grandmother, Mimi. That trophy belonged to my sister, Missy, who was two years older than I.

Ever since I could remember, Missy was Mimi's favorite granddaughter. My mom married my sister's father at eighteen. They quickly divorced, and mom took off for college, leaving Missy to live with her grandparents. Mom then met and married my father, and I arrived two years later. Dad adopted Missy shortly thereafter, and Missy left Mimi's, making us a real family.

From the start, Missy and I were wired differently. She received the quiet, passive genes, while my set of inquisitive, energetic ones led to a personality that burst with exuberance.

When I turned four, my parents divorced, and I started noticing Missy's elevated status with my grandparents. I thought I imagined this discrepancy, until at eight, they chose to take Missy on a Hawaiian vacation. Then at thirteen, Missy cruised the Caribbean with them and came home with a ten-stone emerald ring, encircling an enormous diamond.

Mimi never addressed the partiality, but I perceived that her silent disapproval of my high-spirited temperament was the reason she left me behind. When I ate, she would peer over her glasses, "It's not socially acceptable to cut your ham that way or to eat so much."

While poolside at Mimi's house, Missy lay still on the raft, but I swam like a fish.

"Could you please not splash me while I swim my laps?" Mimi asked. I think my constant laughing frustrated her the most, "Ladies are quiet," she would remind me.

But it was more what she didn't say, for every time she commented on my behavior, there were twenty more glares that slashed my hope of ever gaining her favor. My unrefined nature refused to conform to her polished image of what was proper.

Still, throughout junior high, I tagged along with Missy when she visited my grandparents—when they invited me. I resigned myself to the fact that they would always prefer my sister, but I thought I could earn Mimi's acceptance by mimicking Missy's ladylike conduct. Nothing worked. I carefully monitored my actions, but Mimi's displeasure with my disposition never ceased.

I don't remember when I stopped trying to earn her support, but by the time I reached high school, I didn't visit my grandparents often. I did, however, detect a softening toward me when Mimi asked, "What are your plans after high school?"

Missy had just flunked out of college. Our grandparents had given her a car and funds to attend the educational institution of her choice.

I remember thinking, *Now, after all these years you notice me? Well, I have made it on my own, and I don't need your attention or money.*

Meanwhile, I enrolled in the same university my grandfather had attended. My dad assisted me with tuition, and I worked to offset my expenses. Mimi's flicker of regard for my activities flamed into an inferno of interest with care packages filled with clothes and extra money. She wrote and called me weekly, and I grew to treasure her encouragement, even if it came late.

But her attention wasn't enough to fill the void in my heart. Then, one day, someone invited me to church. For the first time, I heard that God loved me unconditionally and that, if I'd admit I was a sinner and invite Him into my life, He would extend His grace to me, and I could have a real, personal relationship with Him.

Sign me up baby!

After giving Christ my life, I thought all my insecurity would vanish. Yet when I made the college cheerleading squad, I scrambled to Mimi's home to share my victory. *She will really think I am wonderful for such an honor. This will cement any gap in our relationship.*

When I arrived and shared my news, Mimi took me out to the porch, her eyes streaming with tears. "I have wanted to tell you something for a long time."

I had never seen her cry.

"I was wrong to treat you so wretchedly when you were growing up," she said. "You have attained everything that I ever wanted, and the only thing I gave you was criticism. Can you forgive me? You are a delight, cheerleader or not."

I hugged her, swallowing my own cries, "Oh, Mimi, yes. Thank you."

Joni Eareckson Tada said, "God permits what He hates in order to accomplish what He loves."

That is what He did in my life. Because I wasn't indulged with my grandparents' gifts, I developed a strong work ethic. Their obvious displeasure of me hurt, and I never understood why they didn't love me as much as my sister. But my grandmother's apology erased those years of silent disapproval; they didn't matter anymore.

A humble woman and her needy granddaughter grew up together that sunny spring day on the porch. And I can't help but think that God smiled.

Dear Lord, forgiveness is the key to unlocking a bitter heart from bondage. Give me the strength to open this door that has held me a prisoner with my own anger. Show me how to extend Your grace to others. Amen.

Steps

Eva Marie Everson

Now, dear lady, I am not writing you a new command but one we have had from the beginning. I ask that we love one another.

2 John 1:5

My grandmother was not my grandmother—well, not really. She was the wife of my mother's father; they married six months before I was born. Though I was named for my "real" grandmother, Eva, it was at Eunice's knee that I learned some of life's most valuable lessons.

When I was a young girl, I stayed with Grandmother two weeks of my summer vacation from school. These were the two most precious weeks of my year, even more special than Christmas break.

Grandmother, the epitome of Southern gentility, served me breakfast in bed every morning. Not just any breakfast! I ate fruit from crystal champagne glasses, eggs from fine china, and toast buttered with sterling butter knives. Grandmother insisted that I be treated like a princess, ensuring that I would also act like one.

It was Grandmother who, during lunch one afternoon, instructed me, "Close your mouth. Now chew." It was Grandmother who taught me about proper speech, sitting like a lady, tea parties, and satin and lace. It was Grandmother who taught me never to be ashamed of my relationship with God.

One afternoon, when it was hotter in the house than outside its doors, we sat rocking in the large, front porch rockers. Grandmother fanned herself with a hand-held church fan. As always, she wore a beautiful, form-fitting, belted dress, stockings, and dress pumps. Her neck was adorned with pearls, and matching "ear-bobs" were clipped onto the lobes of her ears.

"Grandmother?" I asked, my rocker keeping rhythm with hers. "Do you love Jesus?"

She didn't have to think twice. "Yes siree-bob!" she declared with conviction.

Grandmother taught me one of the most important lessons of my life: that what is not bound by blood is bound in love. Not having the same bloodline did not stop her from loving me unconditionally. I was her granddaughter. Period.

Many years later, when I married, my husband gave me two stepchildren, Christopher and Ashley, as a wedding gift. Loving these children was not something I had to think about doing or decide to do. Though I never have tried to take their mother's place, it is as natural for me to love them as if I had given birth to them myself. When I did give birth to a daughter, Jessica, I determined that she would never be given any special treatment above her half-siblings. In fact, the first rule I declared was that the children would never refer to themselves as half-siblings but as brother and sisters.

"Do you know what I love about you?" Christopher asked me one evening.

"My charm and quick wit?" I teased.

"Besides that," he smirked. "What I love about you is that you have never made Ash and me feel any different than Jess."

I smiled knowingly. "That began with a great lady," I informed him, "who treated me with the love all children deserve, in spite of the blood that does or does not run through their veins."

Grandmother lives in a nursing home now. Stricken with Alzheimer's, she no longer remembers me. I send her cards often, not because I hope for recognition, but because it brings her pleasure. I want her to be full of joy and happiness during her last days on earth. She is, you see, my grandmother.

Dear Lord, teach me to love those people whom You have given to me. Show me how to invest my life into theirs. For love does not consist of only holding a hand but holding a heart. May I hold close the hearts of those I love. Amen.

Thank You, Mom

*A mother's best gift is an
attitude of gratitude.*

Anonymous

Circle of Love

Birdie L. Etchison

*A gift opens the way for the giver and
ushers him into the presence of the great.*

Proverbs 18:16

Mother's Day was coming, and once again I began
looking for a suitable gift.

The year I was five, I presented my mother with
flowers that had impossibly short stems. Later there
were cards with large scrawled letters, drawings with
stick figures, plaster-of-Paris knickknacks that broke
easily, and lopsided cakes with runny icing.

There were dresses that didn't fit, scarves that didn't
suit, nightgowns that weren't practical.

I had to come up with an original idea for this year's
gift. But what? Now that I am a mother, I can

empathize with all that she must have gone through raising her family. And the sudden realization hits: There is nothing that I could give that would ever show how much I love and appreciate my mother.

I remember those hours she spent laboring over the old treadle sewing machine, making costumes for a recital, frilly dresses for Easter, gowns for special parties.

There were elaborate birthday cakes each year— then lessons in ironing, dusting and waxing, bed making, and window washing. Later I learned to make a "perfect" flaky pie crust and knead bread dough to just the right consistency.

I recall the night vigil beside my bed following a tonsillectomy and the times I was held close after a nightmare.

Mother, those were indeed labors of love. How can I ever repay you? How can I express how much it all meant—how much I love you?

The door opens and my own five-year-old Sarah comes in with—what's this—a bouquet of dandelions with impossibly short stems? And there's a smile on her face, a look of pure enchantment, for she is bringing me the best present she can think of.

And as I take the dandelions with sticky stems, I look for just the right vase for this gift. *And now I know, Mom, now I know. It wasn't the dandelions you were accepting; it was me. You weren't receiving a gift; you were giving one. I now must do the same for my daughter. By example I will teach her just as you taught me. And if she should have a child someday, I pray our circle of love, our circle of acceptance, will continue unbroken.*

Dear Lord, my feeble attempts to thank You must look like dandelions with short, sticky stems. But You love me anyway. You have given the gift of acceptance, despite my defects and flaws. I am Your child, and I can always come to You. Thank You for the privilege. Amen.

My Very First E-Mail

D. J. Note

*I have no greater joy than to hear that
my children are walking in the truth.*

3 John 1:4

"But, Mom, all I need is telephone line and a jack," my fifteen-year-old son repeated for the third time.

"Later, Clay," I insisted, "after fair week is over." His six-foot frame slumped in disappointment.

My daughter was taking her 4-H hog to the county fair, and last-minute details crowded my mind. I rechecked my list: show clothes, hair accessories, brush, show number, shampoo (to bathe her hog), towels, ice chest, sandwiches, chips, soda pop, record book, exhibitor's pass. We were preparing for the fair, but all my son could think about was e-mail! He launched his second attack.

"I'll do everything." He sweetened the deal, ambushing me with his boyish grin. "After fair week, you've got that five-day conference up North. That's another week to wait." My mind swirled in a whirlpool of thought while I sorted through the dirty laundry.

"Just say yes," he begged. Secretly, I wanted e-mail too. I was the only member of my writer's group without it. My husband promised to get to it, but his work had taken him out of town. I certainly didn't have the time to bother with it then.

"Mom?" Clay's voice snapped me back to reality.

"OK!" I gave in. "Just don't bother me with details. I'm only one person." My arms straightened as I held his sister's soiled fair jeans in my hands. I took a deep breath, blowing it out slowly, lifting my bangs in a wave of surrender. I tried to erase the frown that had crept onto my face. Clay pasted a juicy kiss on my cheek and flew out the laundry-room door. A muffled "YES!" echoed from the hall.

True to his promise, Clay didn't worry me about the details. He arranged for a friend to help him with the installation of the phone line and jack. He installed the disk on my computer, completing the task in no time. By late the next evening, his one-track mind again raced at full throttle.

"E-mail's set up, Mom!" he hollered. "Why don't you try it out?"

"Look, babe," I said softly. "I've been staring at three hundred hogs since six o'clock this morning." I edged around his large frame, making my way to the kitchen. "It's eleven o'clock. By six o'clock tomorrow morning, I'll be back at the hogs again."

He wouldn't give up. "Just check your e-mail, Mom."

"What's the point?" I asked, slapping together PB and J sandwiches for the next day's lunch and dinner. "Nobody knows my address, Clay!" I thought about my daughter's once-again-soiled show clothes and the seemingly endless stack of sandwiches waiting to be wrapped.

"You never know, Mom," he persisted. "Might be something important there." Clay ushered me to the familiar gray-tweed computer chair. My blurry eyes strained to focus on the screen while I sat in silence, plunking at the computer keys. I didn't want to be angry. I just wanted a good night's sleep. Why couldn't my e-mail fanatic understand that?

To my surprise a memo appeared in the message box.

"Now how did that happen?" I asked. "I don't even know my address." Clay's soft blue eyes sparkled with anticipation. Pulling up a chair beside mine, he waited. As I began to read, my waning strength was renewed. A salty tear slid down my cheek. The screen blurred.

Dear Mom,

I am sorry I sometimes talk back and show you disrespect. Please keep helping me get through these teenage years. Sometimes I have a hard time finding my way. I get frustrated because I want to achieve so much for you, Dad, and myself. You've tried so hard with me.

I love you,
Clay

My hand cupped the slender face leaning against my shoulder. The concerns of fair week faded as the midnight hour approached, and my tenderhearted teen explained the "how-tos" of electronic mail.

"E-mail is great," I tearfully whispered. "But you are my blessing."

Dear Lord, thank You for blessing me with my wonderful children. I so enjoy their tender hearts and loving spirits. May they grow in height and in wisdom, but help them to retain their wide-eyed wonder and grateful hearts. Amen.

My Pretty Mama

Shawnee McCarty Fleenor

"Why do you worry about clothes?
See how the lilies of the field grow.
They do not labor or spin. Yet I tell you
that not even Solomon in all his splendor
was dressed like one of these."

Matthew 6:28-29

My first memory of my mother is so vivid I can almost reach out to touch her pretty face.

We were living on a ranch in the rolling hills of northern New Mexico, isolated but not alone—we were family. I was three years old and an imaginative dreamer, playing dress-up that morning with fancy shoes and wisps of shimmery things from Mama's dresser. I heard her voice calling me to the living room, and there on the coffee table she had prepared a perfect tea party, just for the two of us. There were miniature sandwiches cut into triangles, just the right size for my pudgy hands, and shiny apple wedges beside strips of carrots and peanut-butter-filled celery. The most wonderful part by far was that she had brought out her hand-painted china cups and saucers with their delicate swirls of wild roses and gold edging. I was on my best behavior, a tiny lady sitting beside the most beautiful woman in the world.

Twenty-two years later, no woman was more beautiful at my wedding than my mother. Still a natural brunette in her fifties, Mama's bright blue eyes and lovely smile were showcased by her gold filigree earrings and emerald green suit dress. It was a special dress, more special than she knew.

Mama had been concerned all spring over what she would wear as mother of the bride. A dear friend had given me a gorgeously detailed wedding dress with a full cathedral train. I had chosen inexpensive yet formal dresses for my attendants, and my groom and his attendants wore rented tuxedos. Knowing my delight over these lovely things, Mama felt even the nicest of her dresses would embarrass me as "shabby," though I assured her over and over I would be proud of her no matter what she wore.

I began to suspect Mama hesitated to spend the money for a new dress because she wanted to help us as much as possible with the cost of the wedding. When I shared that with Rob, my fiancé, he suggested we send her the money he'd received for preaching one day at the tiny church where I served as Sunday morning pianist. I laughed and said, "She'd just send it right back!" He insisted, so we conspired to send the money secretly.

We composed a letter, urging Mama to "buy a special dress for this important day that you've prayed over since Shawnee's birth." We mailed the letter along with the check to friends in Illinois near the community where Daddy had preached before he and Mama moved to Colorado, and the couple sent it on to Mama through a money order. They were happy to scheme along with us and even had the bank teller sign the money order in case Mama were to read the signature.

Three days later, Mama called me mid-morning. Her voice was full of excitement, and I knew she wanted to share the news of the surprise "anonymous" letter, but she held back and merely mentioned she thought she would buy a new dress after all.

I could not have been more proud of her the day of the wedding. The dress she had chosen complimented her gentle elegance perfectly with its lacy ecru collar and double-breasted jacket. In the dressing room as I sat in the midst of my wedding finery and Mama's eyes began to mist, I quickly diverted her attention by complimenting her emerald suit. She brightened and leaned over to whisper in my ear, "Someone sent me money anonymously and specifically requested I use it for this." I smiled.

When I look back through my wedding photos, I still think the mother of the bride far outshone the bride herself. And in her fifties, my mother is still every bit as lovely as the young woman in her twenties who filled her daughter's days with tea parties and girl talk.

Dear Lord, I love to give of myself to those I love. What greater joy can I have than to know that I somehow made a difference in their lives. And even when my kindness has no effect on the recipient, it somehow changes me. Thank You for opportunities to give—especially to ones who have given so much to me. Amen.

Thanksgiving for Moms, Every Day

Barbara A. Vogelgesang

I thank my God every time I remember you.

Philippians 1:3

An old friend of mine called to chat recently and wish me a happy Thanksgiving. I've known her since my BC days (before children) and even before my BJ days (before Jim, my husband). She was going on about how successful she and her husband are and how much freedom they have because they chose not to get "bogged down" by a family. They live in Florida and enjoy a very comfortable life. I said, "You have a lot to be thankful for."

"What are you thankful for little mommy," she asked, "the runny noses, extra laundry, sleepless nights, loss of privacy, or loss of identity?" She laughed.

I realized we had traveled very different roads in life and knew she'd never understand . . . loss of identity! I thank the Lord He called me to such a high purpose!

I am so thankful for my family. I remember the days my arms ached to hold my baby. Those sleepless nights nursing, holding, calming my children gave me time to pray, reflect, and relish a truly intimate moment with my babies and God that I would have otherwise missed. I continually seek to see beyond the piles of laundry and runny noses to the first "mama," to the spontaneous "I love you" and a sticky kiss. I thank God for being able to share in the sheer joy of life.

Children don't miss the joy, and I am blessed to learn it again. Through Nicholas and Libby, I've learned about God's unconditional love. I love them even when they tear the house down, and they love me even when I lose my temper. I've found more to love about my husband; what a gift Jim is to my life. Seeing my husband hold and care for and play with our children has helped me see another side of him. Nicholas and Libby have led me to other moms— another blessing, all those new friends and fellow travelers on this journey. God provides again.

"What do I have to be thankful for?" The list is endless. It is my prayer that every mom can see past the job and see the calling of motherhood. It is something to be thankful for, not just on Thanksgiving but unceasingly.

Dear Lord, what do I have to be thankful for? Everything. Thank You for my family and my children and for the joy of motherhood. I wouldn't trade it for any vacation or so-called freedom. For with my children, I am free to love, to teach, and to grow as a person. Thank You for this incredible opportunity. Amen.

Endnotes

"Get the Kid" from *God Uses Cracked Pots* by Patsy Clairmont, a Focus on the Family book published by Tyndale House Publishers. Copyright © 1991 by Patsy Clairmont. All rights reserved. International copyright secured. Used by permission.

Poem "I Can't" in Eva Marie Everson's story, "I Can," is used by permission of the estate of Edgar A. Guest.

About the Compiler

Linda Evans Shepherd is the award-winning author of eleven books including *Teatime Stories for Women* (Honor Books), *Heart-Stirring Stories of Love* (Broadman and Holman), and *Encouraging Hands, Encouraging Hearts* (Servant). She is a member of the National Speakers Association and the Christian Leaders and Speakers Seminar (CLASS) and is heard coast-to-coast on her nationally syndicated radio show, *Right to the Heart*™. As a speaker, Linda makes her audiences laugh and cry as she shares her own stories. She reminds us how to *Tame the Grump,* and that *God Wants Spiritual Fruit, Not Religious Nuts.* She also teaches *How to Make Time* for our friends, family, and a relationship with God. She has been married for over twenty years and has two children.

Linda may be available for your next retreat or special event.

To check Linda's availability, go online to http://www.sheppro.com or call Shepherd Productions at 1-800-755-7007. To hear her or find out more about her show, visit righttotheheart.com.

Do you have a story of friendship or Christmas to tell for a future book? If so, please send it to Linda at:

Teatime Stories
Attn: Linda Evans Shepherd
P.O. Box 6421
Longmont, CO 80501

Or e-mail (paste the text of your e-mail to Linda at): Lswrites@aol.com (We do not accept attached files.)

For editorial guidelines, please check Linda's Web page at http://www.righttotheheart.com or send a self-addressed, stamped envelope to the address listed above.

About the Authors

Vickey Banks is the happily married mother of two terrific children, an inspirational speaker with CLASServices, and the author of *Love Letters to My Baby: A Guided Journal for Expectant and New Mothers.* Vicki may be contacted at: vbinokc@aol.com or www.vickeybanks.com.

Nancy Bayless is a seasoned, award-winning writer with articles in several books as well as magazines such as *Decision, Guideposts, Moody,* and *Focus on the Family.* One of her stories was shown on the television program "It's a Miracle."

Andrea Boeshaar lives in Milwaukee, Wisconsin, with her husband and three adult sons. She's written articles and devotional pieces as well as ten novels and three novellas which were published by Barbour Publishing. Visit her Web site at: http://members.aol.com/akbwrites2.

Donna Braymer is a pastor's wife, mother of three sons, piano teacher, and business editor of her local newspaper. She is the author of the Rascal Raccoon series for children. Meet Rascal at www.RascalRaccoon.com or Donna at DCBraymer@aol.com.

Denise Hawkins Camp is a freelance writer from Tennessee. She has written numerous short stories and novellas for women's magazines as well as essays for the book *Heart-Stirring Stories of Love.* Currently she writes a humor column for the National Sisters in Crime newsletter and is the author of *Moonlight Madness,* a romance novel.

Nancy G. Carter is matriarch of seventeen, a family she adores! She works part-time, volunteers for her church and the hospital, and is a frequent contributor to a monthly feature of the St. Joseph News Press column, "Young at Heart."

Patsy Clairmont is a popular speaker with "Women of Faith" and best-selling author of several books, including *Sportin' a 'Tude.* She has been married to Les for thirty-five years, and they have two sons, Marty and Jason, and a daughter-in-law, Danya.

Jan Coleman's writing dream began at age ten when she adapted her favorite novel, *Little Women,* into a play for the neighborhood kids. (Her mom's cookies and Kool-Aid saved the day.) Jan went on to write for newspapers and national magazines. You may contact her at jwriter@foothill.net.

Barbara Curtis is mother to eleven, grandmother to five. She has published over four hundred articles in fifty magazines, including *Guideposts, Christian Parenting Today,* and *Focus on the Family* as well as two books about preschoolers. Visit her Web site at www.barbaracurtis.com.

Rosey Dow, best-selling author, writes historical mysteries. Her latest release, *Reaping the Whirlwind,* deals with the Scopes monkey trial of 1925, a small town's quest for publicity that changed the course of a nation. Visit her Web site at www.angelfire.com/de/roseydow/.

Judy L. Dudley is a freelance writer living in East Texas with her husband, David, and five children. She has had articles published in *ParentLife* magazine and publishes a women's newsletter. She enjoys singing, quilting, and creating scrapbooks.

Wendy Dunham is a wife, a mom, an author, and a registered therapist for differently-abled children. When she's not playing with her children, gardening, or doing laundry, she can be found at her computer writing! Wendy may be contacted at: 3148 Lake Rd., Brockport, NY 14420. (716) 637-0535.

Carla Edmisten enjoys writing about life with her daughter, Shelby, and son, Logan. She and her husband, Jeff, make their home near Fredericksburg, Virginia, where Carla is active in her church and in their investigative business.

Birdie L. Etchison, residing on the lovely Pacific coast, currently writes for the inspirational romance line. She teaches for Writer's Digest School, conducts writing seminars, and has been codirector of Writer's Weekend at the Beach for the past nine years.

Eva Marie Everson, a noted speaker and teacher, is the author of *True Love: Engaging Stories of Real-Life Proposals,* and *One True Vow* (Promise Press.) She is the coauthor of *Pinches of Salt, Prisms of Light* (Essence, 1999) and a contributing author to a number of publications. She and her husband have three children and a new grandchild. Eva Marie may be contacted at: 407-695-9366.

Shawnee McCarty Fleenor is a writer, speaker, and minister's wife living with her brilliant, handsome husband, Rob, in Nevada, Missouri.

She is the author of eighty articles and short stories in Christian and mainstream publications, including *Today's Christian Woman*.

Jo Franz enjoys being a wife, stepmother, grandmother, writer, and speaker for banquets, retreats, and conferences. She weaves songs from her CDs into each presentation. Her stories appear in a number of books as well as *Decision* magazine. You may contact Jo at Jofranz@aol.com.

Nancy B. Gibbs is a pastor's wife and the mother of three grown children. She is a weekly religion columnist and a freelance writer. She has been published by Honor Books and Guideposts and in several magazines and devotional guides.

Anne Marie Goodrich is the mother of three wonderful children—two college students and a fifth grader. She is also a full-time Web designer for an educational institution in Kalamazoo, Michigan, and devotes her spare time to writing and working on her personal e-card Web site, OhAngel.com.

N. C. Haas is the pen name under which the author submits this true story. She is a freelance writer living in Southern California and can be contacted through WORDable SOLUTIONS at (714) 775-6705 or by e-mail at armhumber@aol.com.

Bonnie Compton Hanson is author of several books for adults and children, as well as poems, stories, and articles. She is also a joyous mom and grandmom. You may contact her at 3330 S. Lowell St., Santa Ana, CA 92707; (714) 751-7824; e-mail: bonnieh1@worldnet.att.net.

D. Harrison is an internationally published poet. She is the author of *Shared Journey* and *North of the Sky*. Her new book *Walking in New Given Strength* will be released in October of 2000 from Wings of Dawn Publishing.

Elizabeth Hey is a freelance writer and member of Kansas City Christian Writer's Network. As a homeschooling mother of two sons and a daughter, ages twelve, nine, and six, she says the Lord often teaches her life's lessons through her children.

Deborah Holt enjoys writing poetry and short inspirational essays. She is a mother of three and a grandmother of one. In her very little free time, she indulges her quiet passion for reading, strong coffee, and good conversation.

Mary van Balen Holt is an author, columnist, and educator. Her books include *Marriage: A Covenant of Seasons,* and *A Dwelling Place Within.* Mary gives presentations on spirituality and prayer. She is married and is the mother of three.

Betty J. Johnson, inspirational writer and speaker, lives with her husband in colorful Colorado, surrounded by her three married children and nine grandchildren. She also enjoys golfing, leading small groups, and mentoring.

Dr. Linda Karges-Bone currently prepares future teachers at Charleston Southern University, in Charleston, South Carolina. She is the author of twenty-two books, fifty-five children's stories, and hundreds of scholarly and popular articles. Linda is the creator and host of *Prayerful Parenting,* a radio program heard through the Family Radio Network. Married for twenty years to Gary R. Bone, a biomedical engineer, and the mother of two daughters, ages thirteen and sixteen, Linda lives with her family in coastal South Carolina.

Nancy Kennedy lives in Inverness, Florida, with her husband, Barry, and youngest daughter, Laura. Her most recent books are *Prayers God Always Answers* and *Move Over Victoria, I Know the Real Secret* (WaterBrook Press).

Patricia Lorenz is the author of *Stuff That Matters for Single Parents* and *A Hug a Day for Single Parents.* She is a contributing writer for ten of the *Chicken Soup for the Soul* books, has had over four hundred articles published, and is a regular columnist for two newspapers. For speaking engagements, phone Associated Speakers at 1-800-437-7577 or e-mail her at: patricialorenz@juno.com.

Nancy Maffeo is a homemaker, mother of three, and freelance writer. She lives with her husband and youngest son in San Diego, California. She has taught elementary school in the United States and Japan.

Donna McDonnall is a freelance Christian writer and registered nurse from Lamar, Colorado. She and her husband, Bruce, have three grown children. Donna has had several articles published in newspapers, books, and magazines. You may contact her at mcdonnal@ria.net.

DiAnn Mills is the author of short stories, articles, devotions, two novellas, and four novels and contributor for seven anthologies. She is a founding board member and treasurer of American Christian

Romance Writers. DiAnn may be contacted at: 14410 Dracaena Court, Houston, Texas 77070, or millsdg@flash.net. Web site: www.rehobothministries.com.

Marilyn Mohr's stories are based on personal experiences and reflect the help of our Lord in difficult situations. She recently retired from twenty-five years of teaching elementary school and is currently writing some of her life stories.

D. J. Note is the mother of two teenagers, a member of Oregon Christian Writers and Mom's in Touch Int'l., and a regular contributor to *Cascade Horseman* magazine. Her love of God, family, and country life inspire her writing. D. J. may be contacted at: djnote@integrityonline.com.

Golden Keyes Parsons, Matters of the Heart Ministries, is a CLASS speaker, writer, and musician who enjoys speaking at women's events. She ministers with her husband at Faith Mountain Fellowship in Red River, New Mexico. For booking information, call (505) 754-1742 or e-mail GPar0719@aol.com.

Deborah Raney's first novel, *A Vow to Cherish* was the inspiration for World Wide Pictures' highly acclaimed film of the same title. Her newest novel is *Beneath a Southern Sky.* Deborah and her husband, author and illustrator Ken Raney, have four children and live in Kansas. Visit Deborah at www2.southwind.net/debraney.

Carol McAdoo Rehme is a four-time mom who has kissed skinned knees and baby dolls, bathed puppies and cowboys (sometimes together), nursed chicken pox and teen heartache. Her new life-after-kids includes a career as a professional storyteller and freelance writer. Contact her at crehme@verinet.com.

Suzy Ryan lives in Southern California with her family. Her articles have appeared in *Decision, Today's Christian Woman, Christian Parenting Today, Woman's World, The American Enterprise, Bounce Back Too, Stories for a Teen's Heart,* and various newspapers. You can reach her at KenSuzyR@aol.com.

Dee Sanger-Hyatt shares her life with her husband, Ted. They are parents of three dogs and two cats. She is currently finishing her first novel for children. Dee may be contacted at: 619 Curve Circle Lancaster, CA 93535 (661) 942-8858; veilshome@cs.com.

Margie Seyfer conducts workshops on attitude enhancement and keynote speeches. You may contact her at Seyfermarg@aol.com for her book, *From Attitude to Zeal–26 Insights for Energizing Your Life.*

Joy Shelton is a speaker, freelance writer, and encourager from Winter Garden, Florida. She is the founder and director of Sprinkles of Joy Ministries, a Personality Plus trainer, and a member of CLASS. Joy has been a minister's wife for thirty plus years.

Joyce Simmons is an exciting author and conference speaker, challenging and motivating people to be all they can be in their daily walks with God. She is the founder of Dynamic Family Ministries, conducting seminars on family issues. She and her husband, Bill, are also involved in working with other ministries to see their vision fulfilled.

Sara L. Smith is a freelance writer with over two hundred published articles and short stories. She also works part time as a medical office receptionist. Sara and her husband, Ron, live in Virginia and have five children and three grandchildren.

Rhonda Wheeler Stock lives in Kansas with her husband and four children. Her work has appeared in *Today's Christian Woman, Moody, The Kansas City Star,* and other publications. Rhonda is available for retreats, women's meetings, and youth groups.

Julie Sutton, homeschooling mother of two, is author of the popular Just Us Girls humorous gift books and greeting cards. Former Hallmark senior editor, she writes for a variety of publishers, such as Zondervan, Tyndale House, Garborg's, and DaySpring.

Judith A. Wiegman is a storytelling speaker and author. A one-of-a-kind communicator, Judi speaks with knowledge and skill coupled with passion and creativity. She is available to share her renewed life in Christ at retreats and other functions. Contact 4520 Keys Dr., The Colony, TX 75056; (972) 625-6420; ScarletCrd@aol.com.

Bobbie Wilkinson, a freelance writer, artist, and musician, is also the "Spirit and Song leader" at Camp Mom in Southern California. She has three grown daughters and lives with her husband in a self-renovated barn in the northern Virginia countryside. Bobbie can be reached at bobbiewilkinson@earthlink.net.

Additional copies of this book and other titles
compiled by Linda Evans Shepherd are
available from your local bookstore.

Teatime Stories for Women

If you have enjoyed this book or if it has impacted
your life, we would like to hear from you.

Please contact us at:

RiverOak Publishing
Department E
P. O. Box 700143
Tulsa, OK 74170-0143

RIVER
OAK

PUBLISHING